Business Plan Project

Business Plan Project

A Step-by-Step Guide to Writing a Business Plan

David Sellars, PhD

First published in 2009 by
Business Expert Press, LLC
222 East 46th Street, New York, NY 10017
www.businessexpertpress.com

ISBN-13: 978-1-60649-110-2 (paperback)
ISBN-10: 1-60649-110-5 (paperback)

ISBN-13: 978-1-60649-111-9 (e-book)
ISBN-10: 1-60649-111-3 (e-book)

DOI 10.4128/9781606491119

A publication in the Business Expert Press Small Business Management and Entrepreneurship collection

Collection ISSN: 1946-5653 (print)
Collection ISSN: 1946-5661 (electronic)

Cover design by Artistic Group—Monroe, NY
Interior design by Scribe, Inc.

First edition: October 2009

10 9 8 7 6 5 4 3 2 1

Printed in the United States of America.

I wish to dedicate this book to Judy, my life partner.

Abstract

Business Plan Project provides detailed instructions on how to write a comprehensive business plan for new ventures. The intended market segments are graduate or upper-level undergraduate students, entrepreneurs, consultants, and college instructors or corporate trainers. *Business Plan Project* can be used in executive development programs and over 10 college-level courses.

Business Plan Project is designed to meet important needs of each segment: (1) the business plan serves as a means for college students to learn about the major functions of business and how they are interrelated, (2) entrepreneurs need a business plan to provide direction in the organization and launch of a new business and secure initial capital from funding sources, (3) consultants need a user-friendly business plan format to assist clients that have limited or no business experience, and (4) instructors and trainers need a turn-key text with supplements that require no lecture and little prep time to teach students how to write a business plan.

Business Plan Project is a real-world, hands-on, step-by-step guide where students or entrepreneurs develop business plans for new ventures. The experience begins with brainstorming and deciding on a new business that meets the unique needs in the marketplace. It ends with writing a comprehensive business plan and conducting a PowerPoint presentation of the plan. Further realism is achieved through the use of a continuing case: AVID SPORTS, INC., a start-up company that plans to launch a high performance running shoe called "Propell." All concepts in the text are explained using AVID as an example.

The instructor's manual includes outcomes for the learning experience, assessment methods, lesson plans, teaching ideas, test bank, financial statement worksheets, and forms to grade the written plan and oral presentation of the plan. Since all information that students need to develop professional business plans is in the text, lectures, handouts, and other learning aids are optional. The instructor's role can be that of a consultant to students.

Business Plan Project has been thoroughly tested by students and entrepreneurs and can be offered as an e-book for domestic and international markets.

Keywords

Executive development, business plan, business plan simulation, business simulation, organization plan, marketing plan, financial plan, new ventures, new businesses, new business ideas, entrepreneur, small business management, business strategy, business analysis, industry analysis, competitive analysis, and financial analysis

Contents

Preface

To the Entrepreneur

Business Plan Project will take you on an exciting journey into the world of opportunities open to you as an entrepreneur. More than a technical "how-to" manual, *Business Plan Project* is an interactive tool that allows you to assume the role of the entrepreneur and to create a plan for a new business from concept to fruition.

The trip begins when you conceive of an idea for a new product, service, retail store, or restaurant. Then, with you in the driver's seat, you will make decisions regarding a name for the company, how it will be staffed, a desirable location, and what equipment is needed to make your dream a reality. Using marketing strategies, you will outline ways to bring consumers through your door. You will also prepare financial statements to take you all the way to the bank.

Down the road, your brainchild will be showcased as you create a business plan and present your ideas in a dynamic oral presentation to maximize success.

Business Plan Project is intended to challenge both your academic and creative energies. Enjoy the experience.

David Sellars, PhD

To the Instructor

Overview

Business Plan Project is a real-world, hands-on, step-by-step guide where students develop business plans for new ventures. The experience begins with students brainstorming and deciding on a new business that meets a unique need in the marketplace. It ends with students writing comprehensive business plans and conducting PowerPoint presentations of the plans. Throughout the experience, students assume the role of entrepreneurs.

Further realism is achieved through the use of a continuing case: AVID SPORTS, INC., a start-up company that plans to launch a high-performance running shoe called "Propell." Students get an insider's view of how the founders intend to establish the company and write their business plan. All concepts in the text are explained using AVID as an example, and the content of all sections of AVID's business plan are presented so students can see what they contain.

Another unique feature is that the instructor can create a competitive environment in class, which will provide additional motivation among students to create the best plans. At the beginning of the learning experience, students are told they are developing their plans for a group of potential investors that could provide start-up capital to launch their businesses. Students compete for this fictitious funding. Rubrics in the instructor's manual for the written plan and oral presentation of the plan can be used to determine the winners. A certificate or special recognition could be given to students who develop the best plans.

Courses, Skills, and Knowledge

Business Plan Project is designed to be a primary text in a 7- or 10-week accelerated course or a supplement in a semester course. It is written for any experience where students learn about the major functions of a business and how these functions are interrelated. The following are courses and programs that are ideally suited for the learning experience provided in *Business Plan Project*:

- Entrepreneurship
- New Venture Planning
- Small Business Management
- Business Strategy
- Strategic Business
- Business Capstone
- Executive Development

The text is designed to develop the following skills:

- Creative thinking
- Critical thinking
- Secondary and primary research
- Business situation analysis
- Identification of strengths, weaknesses, opportunities, and threats (SWOTs)
- Financial analysis
- Report writing
- Oral presentation skills

Detailed learning outcomes are noted at the beginning of each chapter in *Looking Ahead* sections. They identify more specific skills and knowledge that students will gain.

Structure

Students complete each of the chapters of the business plan sequentially. Questions at the end of chapters ask students to record information for a chapter. Chapter content provides the knowledge needed to write the section. Completing one chapter before proceeding to the next keeps students involved and their time and effort are spread over the entire learning experience. Instructors can assess students' work and provide input along the way.

Content

There are four major parts to the business plan: opportunity analysis, organization plan, marketing plan, and financial plan. All information needed to complete each part of the plan is in the text. Each chapter includes learning outcomes, content related to the section of the plan, examples related to the AVID SPORTS continuing case, a list of key concepts discussed (which are in italic font in the body of the chapter), and questions students address; answers to these questions serve as the content of their plans.

For entrepreneurs with limited business experience and students, the most challenging section of a business plan is the financial plan. A considerable amount of time went into researching, writing, and revising this chapter. There are five critical elements that were used to make the development of financial statements manageable for students.

First, some assumptions are made about financial issues and are explained in the text. This significantly reduces the complexity of financial statements. Second, an extensive list of costs for equipment and leasing space for an office, retail store, and restaurant is provided. Third, the financial statements' items are discussed and expressed in a clear manner. Fourth, examples of all financial statements are provided for the AVID case. And finally, instructional worksheets are provided to help students construct each statement in a step-by-step manner. These worksheets, which can be given to students, are in the instructor's manual. A student doesn't have to be an expert in accounting or finance to create professional financial statements.

The last chapter explains in detail what information is to be included in the written plan and the PowerPoint presentation of the plan.

Instructor's Manual

A great deal of time was spent developing the instructor's manual. It includes outcomes for the learning experience, assessment methods, information on how to effectively use teams, lesson plans, content that can be included in the syllabus, teaching ideas, a test bank, financial statement worksheets, and rubrics to grade the written and oral presentation of the plan.

Contact the publisher, david.parker@businessexpertpress.com, to secure a copy of the instructor's manual. Verification that you are an instructor at an educational institution will be needed.

Learning Options

Business Plan Project provides an opportunity to customize the learning experience given the desired outcomes of the course. The three options that can be used are listed on the next page and discussed in the instructor's manual.

- Students develop business plans individually.
- Teams of students develop plans.
- Time is allotted during the semester for the business plan unit (either limited, moderate, or extensive).

Since all information that students need to develop professional business plans is in the text, lectures, handouts, and other learning aids are optional. The instructor's role can be that of a consultant to students. During class, students can discuss their progress and challenges, share their findings, and solicit input from other students and the instructor. If the course involves another textbook and lecture, *Business Plan Project* will reinforce and significantly extend learning.

INTRODUCTION

Entrepreneurs and the Business Plan

Looking Ahead

Upon completion of this chapter, you should be able to

1. describe the role of the entrepreneur;
2. discuss the importance of the business plan;
3. explain the business plan project including how it is organized and the activities involved;
4. identify and evaluate innovative business concepts for new products, services, retail stores, and restaurants; and
5. write and evaluate business concept statements.

Chapter Overview

The purpose of this chapter is to explain the role of the entrepreneur in our economy and to provide an overview of the business plan project. You will also learn how to get started forming a business. The following topics are presented in this chapter:

- The Role of the Entrepreneur
- The Business Plan Project
- Overview of the Business Plan
- Identifying Innovative Business Concepts

The Role of the Entrepreneur

What do Michael Dell, Maxiane Clark, and Gordon Bowker have in common? They are entrepreneurs. *Entrepreneurs* are people who form, own, and operate businesses.

Michael Dell began his business while still a freshman at the University of Texas. He built computers in his dormitory based on customer specifications and sold them by mail. Today, Dell Computers is one of the largest computer manufacturers in the world.

Maxiane Clark was president of a national shoe retailer and was looking for a new challenge. She conducted focus groups with children and came up with the idea where children would stuff, dress, and accessorize their own teddy bears in a store. Build-A-Bear Workshop was formed. It has over 150 outlets in the United States and many new stores are planned.

Gordon Bowker loved coffee and—with the help of his friends, Jerry Baldwin and Zev Siegl—developed a blend from special beans that produced a dark, full-bodied coffee. Starbucks was formed and currently has more coffee cafés than any firm in the world.

Over 1 million people each year become entrepreneurs. They are motivated to do so for several reasons. They want to pursue something in which they have interest and want to create something new. They want to be their own bosses and to achieve success. The possibility of high income can also be a factor. Owning a business has its drawbacks, however. There is a great deal of risk involved. For every successful new business there are many that fail. Entrepreneurs must spend long hours at work to make the business successful. Income may be uncertain during the first 2 or 3 years of operation, as well.

The following personal qualities are needed to be a successful entrepreneur:

- Ability to recognize unsatisfied needs that may present new business opportunities
- Passion for an idea for a new business
- Free spirit and a desire to be ones own boss
- Intense drive to make things happen
- Ability to set and achieve high goals

- Willingness to assume risk
- Knowledge of the operations, marketing, and finance functions of a business

Throughout this project you will be assuming the role of an entrepreneur.

The Business Plan Project

The experience on which you are about to embark will explore the fascinating world of business. What is it like to be an entrepreneur? How is a business formed? What plans are needed to help ensure success? How do departments in a business function and relate to one another? What does it cost to launch a new business? Where can funds be secured to launch a business?

One of the best ways to answer these questions is to develop a *business plan* for a new venture. This document is a written proposal that describes how the business will be structured and operated during a specified period, typically one or more years. It is like a map to a traveler or a blueprint to a carpenter. You will develop a business plan in this project. Upon completion of the experience, you should be able to

1. prepare and write a business plan for a new venture,
2. develop and deliver an effective oral report of a plan,
3. gather and analyze data and make recommendations based on sound reasoning, and
4. explain important business concepts.

This learning experience begins with brainstorming ideas for new, innovative businesses. The best idea is chosen, and the business plan is developed for this business. Work can then begin on the plan by applying the principles discussed in this book. Each chapter explains a section in the business plan. Questions at the end of the chapters explain what is needed for the plan. At the end of the experience, you will write a report that explains your plans for the business. The process to complete the plan and information in it are the same as what is used by highly successful entrepreneurs.

Throughout this experience, assume that you are developing the plan for potential investors who could provide start-up capital to launch the business. Also assume that you are competing against other students in the class and that investors will fund only one business of those being developed. The business plan that is funded will be determined by which venture has the best business plan.

Overview of the Business Plan

Many new businesses fail during the first 3 to 5 years of operation. Several factors may contribute to a lack of success. One reason is that start-up firms often do not have a business plan. The business plan serves may important functions. First, it is a guide on how to form and operate a company during the period it is being launched. Second, the plan provides strategies to achieve these goals. It is also a means to measure progress. And finally, the business plan can be used to convince banks and potential investors to provide the start-up capital necessary to launch a business. For these reasons, the business plan is perhaps the most important document for a new company.

A business plan contains six sections: the executive summary, opportunity analysis, the organization plan, the marketing plan, the financial plan, and supporting documents and bibliography. The *executive summary* is the introduction to the business plan that provides a concise overview of the proposed business. It highlights the most critical information that bankers and potential investors want to know before investing in a new business. The *opportunity analysis* section provides a review of industry and competitor factors that will impact success. The *organization plan* describes how a firm will be structured and staffed, where it will be located, and what office or retail space it will occupy. Products or services that the firm will offer are outlined in the *marketing plan*. It also describes pricing, distribution, and promotion strategies of the firm. The *financial plan* outlines projected sales revenue, expenses, and profit or loss and details what the firm will own and owe at the end of each year of operation. The *supporting documents and bibliography* is the last section of the business plan. It contains exhibits such as an organizational chart and financial statements and a list of sources that were cited in the plan. These six sections are discussed in this book.

Writing a business plan for the first time is challenging, so an example of a plan is included in this book. AVID SPORTS, INC. ("AVID"), the company that is profiled, is a start-up firm that plans to produce and market a high-performance running shoe called "Propell." The shoe offers a unique feature that is not available in other athletic shoes. The content of the AVID business plan is presented throughout the book. Numerous examples of other business plans can be found at the Web site, http://www.bplans.com.

Identifying Innovative Business Concepts

The first step in this project is to identify an idea for a new business. It can be a company that produces a product or offers a service, or it could be a retail store or restaurant that is not currently being marketed.

There are two common approaches that entrepreneurs use to identify ideas for new businesses. The first involves thinking of unmet consumer needs and wants. You can start by asking yourself, "What unmet needs and wants do I have?" Ask others the same question. Unmet needs exist in all industries. The second approach considers the fact that any product or service can be a solution to a problem. Exploring the question "What problems exist for which there is no product or service that offers a solution?" can reveal a business opportunity.

A method of exploring these questions is called *brainstorming*. This involves recording ideas for new businesses without evaluating the feasibility of ideas. The goal in brainstorming is to come up with as many ideas as possible—even ones that may seem very farfetched. Technology may not yet exist for some ideas. The entrepreneur can be creative and have fun with this technique.

Once ideas have been formulated, a formal *business concept statement* must be written for each idea. This is a written statement that describes the idea for a new venture. The statement must be concise: no more than one sentence. It must also explain to those who are not familiar with the idea what unique feature or benefit is to be offered. Why would potential customers buy it? The following are some examples of business concept statements.

Products

- Voice-activated television remote
- College textbooks on universal serial bus (USB) drives
- Solar-powered cell phone
- Combination clothes washer and dryer in one

Services

- Grocery buying and delivery service
- Psychological counseling service by phone
- Seminar on managing money and credit offered to high school students nationwide

Retail Stores

- Extreme sports store
- Furniture/appliance store that offers products for college dormitory rooms

Restaurants

- Exotic-food restaurant
- Restaurant that projects feature-length movies in the dining area
- Restaurant with computer touch-screens on each table for ordering and surfing the Internet

Note that the statements are very concise and clearly explain the unique feature or benefit offered.

Concepts to Know

brainstorming	marketing plan
business concept statement	opportunity analysis
entrepreneur	organization plan
executive summary	supporting documents and bibliography
financial plan	

Business Plan Issues

1. *Business Concepts.* Study this chapter. Create a list of at least five innovative business concepts that could be the focus of the project and write a concept statement for each. Consider products, services, retail stores, and restaurants that are not currently being marketed. Each concept statement should not exceed one sentence. Be creative.

2. *Concept Approval.* Secure approval from your instructor for the concept that you would most like to have as the focus of your business plan.

3. *Sample Business Plans.* Go to the Web site, http://www.bplans .com. Identify and read one business plan for each of the following: product, service, retail store, and restaurant.

CHAPTER 1

Opportunity Analysis

Looking Ahead

Upon completion of this chapter, you should be able to

1. explain the purpose of the opportunity analysis;
2. analyze an industry, its customers, and its competitors;
3. identify and define a target market;
4. design a questionnaire and conduct a market research study to determine the perceptions and needs of a target market; and
5. analyze results of the research study and make recommendations based on the findings.

Purpose of the Opportunity Analysis

The purpose of the *opportunity analysis* section of the business plan is to determine the probability that a business concept will be successful in the marketplace. It also describes the group of customers that will be the focus of a firm's endeavors. This chapter explains how to develop your plans in the following areas:

- Market Research
- Industry and Customer Analysis
- Competitor Analysis
- Sources of Industry, Customer, and Competitor Information
- Market Segmentation
- Defining a Target Market
- Perceptions and Needs of the Target Market
- Preparing for Team Meetings

Market Research

Determining the future potential of a new business is very important because the entrepreneur does not want to invest time and money in a venture unless success is likely. Market research is used to determine the potential of a new business. *Market research* is the process of gathering and analyzing information about an industry, its customers, and its competitors that will aid in decision making. Companies in the United States spend over $1 billion annually for market research to increase the chances of success.

There are two broad types of market research information: secondary and primary data. *Secondary data* is previously gathered data. There is a great deal of information about industries and businesses that can be found in books, periodicals, government publications, trade manuals, electronic databases, and other sources. Secondary data is gathered before primary data because information needed for decision making may already be available. Securing the information is inexpensive because the only cost is the time spent by the researcher. A list of secondary data sources that can be used for your opportunity analysis is provided later in the chapter.

Primary data is data that is gathered for the first time. A *questionnaire* is generally used to gather data from respondents. *Personal interviews* can be conducted using a questionnaire. They can be face-to-face or on the telephone. One type of personal interview that involves a small group of eight to ten people is called a *focus group*. Respondents are together in a meeting room where the researcher asks questions. *Mail surveys* involve using the postal system to send and receive questionnaires. The Internet is a useful means to distribute a questionnaire and gather primary data. To ensure the results of a survey accurately reflect the opinions of respondents, it is important to carefully choose the sample of people to be surveyed. While the cost to conduct a survey is high, it can provide very relevant information for decision making. The survey that you can conduct for your business plan is discussed later in the chapter.

Industry and Customer Analysis

Before proceeding with a new venture, the entrepreneur must assess external factors that will impact success. This involves conducting an industry, customer, and competitor analysis.

An *industry analysis* describes the size and current trends in the industry. Secondary data is gathered that is related to the following issues:

1. Name of the industry
2. Total current industry sales volume
3. Growth rate of industry sales in the past 3 years
4. Projected industry sales in the next 3 years
5. Recent trends in the industry including product or service innovations, pricing, distribution (how products or services are made available to customers), and promotion (including advertising)

The *customer analysis* describes who purchases *any* products or services in the industry. The profile is not limited to the customers the start-up firm intends to target. Secondary data is reviewed to identify the following information:

1. Number of consumers who purchase *any* products or services in the industry per year
2. Characteristics of consumers who purchase *any* products or services in the industry (age, gender, income, education, and occupation). Of particular interest are characteristics of heavy users of the products or services.

Needs and wants of customers are also determined in the customer analysis. These will be identified in the market research survey that is discussed later.

In the previous chapter, it was mentioned that a continuing case featuring AVID SPORTS is used to illustrate the content of sections in a business plan. AVID is planning to produce and market a high-performance running shoe. The industry and customer analysis of the athletic shoe market that the firm completed is summarized in Exhibit 1.1.

Exhibit 1.1. Industry and Customer Analysis: Athletic Shoe Market

Industry Analysis

Industry: Footwear > athletic shoes > running shoes > high-performance running shoes

Current annual industry sales are as follows:

- *Footwear*: $47 billion
- *Athletic shoes*: $16 billion
- *Running shoes*: $4.8 billion

Running shoes represent 30% of total athletic shoe sales. Sales growth during the past 3 years for athletic shoes has averaged 3.5% per year.

Future sales growth: Projected sales during the next 3 years are expected to be moderate and in the range of 2% to 4% per year. Factors that will increase sales are population increases and the shift away from dress shoes worn in the workplace to casual shoes.

Recent industry trends include the following:

1. *Product innovations*: Production of most athletic shoes sold in the United States is outsourced to overseas firms. There have been very few product innovations in the industry for the past several years.
2. *Pricing*: Many manufacturers are offering wholesalers and retailers deep discounts, which has resulted in the moderation of retail prices. Low- to moderately priced athletic shoes appear to be gaining in popularity.
3. *Distribution*: Manufacturers are expanding distribution by selling athletic shoes directly to consumers on company Web sites.
4. *Promotion*: The use of sports celebrities to endorse brands and sponsoring major sporting events continues to be popular means of promotion. The amount that manufacturers spend in advertising is not expected to increase in the next 3 years.

Exhibit 1.1. (continued)

Customer Analysis

The demographic profile of the consumers who spend the most on athletic shoes is as follows:

1. *Age*: Primary 25–34; secondary 35–54
2. *Gender*: Women buy 20% more athletic shoes then men, however, their purchases are more apt to be for fashion rather than for performance
3. *Income*: Primary $50,000+; secondary $30,000–$49,999 per year
4. *Education*: College degree
5. *Household size*: Families with teenage children
6. *Usage*: Less than 30% of athletic shoe purchases are for use in sports or fitness activities

Competitor Analysis

The *competitor analysis* describes firms that will compete for sales of the proposed business concept. Concepts that are not revolutionary have direct competitors. These are firms that market the same or very similar products or services. New-to-the-world product or service firms, however, must consider companies that offer different but somewhat-related products or services that may compete for the same consumer dollars. These are indirect competitors. For example, a typical sporting goods store would be an indirect competitor to an extreme-sports specialty store. Information required for this section of the business plan is as follows:

1. Company name of the competitor
2. Products or services the competitor sells
3. Past and current company sales (not available for privately owned firms)
4. Brand name of competing product (if different than the company name)
5. Unique product or service features and benefits

6. Price of the products or services
7. Distribution

If the competitor is a producer, you should include the following:
- Types of stores or other businesses that sell the competitor's products
- Number of stores or other businesses that stock the product (one, few, or many in each geographic area)

If the competitor is a service that is visited by customers, a retail store, or a restaurant, you should include the following:
- Number of outlets in the country where the concept could be launched
- Number of outlets in the local area
- Geographic location(s) in the local area
- Days and hours of operation
- Appearance of the store interior and exterior

8. Promotion
- Advertising media used
- Amount of funds invested in advertising (none, limited, or extensive)
- Availability and type of content of a Web site

9. Overall awareness of the product or firm (low, medium, or high)
10. Reputation and image of the product or firm (fair, good, or excellent)

This information is gathered to develop a profile for each competitor. It is then analyzed so that strengths and weaknesses can be identified.

The major competitors in the athletic shoe industry are Nike, Reebok, and Stride Rite. However, AVID has determined that its primary competitor is a small company that markets high-performance running shoes. A profile and analysis of strengths and weaknesses of this competitor are provided in Exhibit 1.2.

Exhibit 1.2. Competitor Analysis for Cheetah Sports, Inc.

Competitor Profile

- *Company name*: Cheetah Sports, Inc. A world-class runner who won two of the top marathon races in the United States founded the company 5 years ago.
- *Products it sells*: Men and women's high-performance running shoes.
- *Past and current sales*: The company is privately owned so actual sales are confidential. Industry experts speculate that annual sales are $8 million. The firm is experiencing a growth rate of approximately 20% per year.
- *Brand name*: Road Claw XL
- *Unique product features*: The shoe was developed and tested by Kinetech Laboratories under the direction of the founder. The technology in the heel of the shoe consists of five foam towers for added cushioning. A special tread on the sole of the shoe provides improved traction. White, gray, and purple color combinations offer a contemporary style. EVA rubber is used for durability. The shoe weighs 12.6 ounces.
- *Price*: $150 suggested retail price
- *Distribution*: Shoes are sold to exclusive sporting goods stores. They are not currently available in discount chain stores.
- *Promotion*: The company has a very limited advertising budget. It runs six ads per year in *Runner's World* magazine. It also has a Web site with product information and a list of stores where the shoe can be purchased.
- *Overall awareness of the company and product*: Awareness is low due to limited funds for advertising.
- *Reputation and image*: The company's reputation is very good among specialty sporting goods store managers and serious runners.

Exhibit 1.2. (continued)

Competitor Strengths and Weaknesses

Characteristic	Strengths	Weaknesses
Company size		X
Running shoe		
Heel technology		X
Sole technology	X	
Fit		X
Styling	X	
Durability		X
Weight	X	
Price	X	
Distribution		X
Promotion		X
Awareness		X
Reputation/image	X	

Sources of Industry, Customer, and Competitor Information

There are many excellent sources that provide information for your industry, customer, and competitor analysis. Some of the most popular ones are presented in the following list. Print sources should be available at your educational institution or public library.

Print Sources

- *Industry Surveys.* Standard & Poor's. New York: Standard & Poor's. Contains industry trends and information on companies. (Industry and competitor analysis)
- *Encyclopedia of Associations.* The Gale Group. Barrington Hills: The Gale Group. Information about trade associations for your industry. Call appropriate associations and request information. (Industry, customer and competitor analysis)

- *Hoover's Handbook of American Business.* Austin, TX: Hoover's Business Press. Contains the histories and sales for hundreds of companies. (Competitor analysis)
- *International Directory of Company Histories.* Detroit, MI: St. James Press. Contains the histories and sales for the hundreds of companies. (Competitor analysis)
- *Standard & Poor's Register of Corporations, Directors & Executives.* Charlottesville, VA: Standard & Poor's. Lists the company addresses and other details. (Competitor analysis)
- *Household Spending: Who Spends How Much on What.* Ithaca, NY: New Strategist Publications. Lists the spending habits for different demographic groups and hundreds of products and services. (Customer analysis)
- *Best Customers: Demographics of Consumer Demand.* Ithaca, NY: New Strategist. Contains information on the best customers for hundreds of products and services. (Customer analysis)
- *Yellow Pages* telephone directory. All companies in your local area listed by type of business. (Competitor analysis)

Electronic Sources

- *CI Strategies and Tools.* Available at http://www.fuld.com/i3/index.html. Contains numerous links to sites with valuable information. (Industry, customer, and competitor analysis)
- *U.S. Small Business Administration.* Available at http://www.sbaonline.sba.gov. Contains economic and industry data for the United States, state, and local area. (Industry analysis)
- *U.S. Census Bureau.* Available at http://www.census.gov. Contains demographic information of consumers for the United States, state, and local area. (Customer analysis)
- *Free demographic Web sites.* Available at http://freedemographics.com and http://ersys.com. Contain consumer demographic data. (Customer analysis)
- *Annual Reports Online.* Available at http://www.zpub.com/sf/arl. Shows how to access financial reports of companies. (Competitor analysis)

- Competitor Web sites
- Search engines such as Google and Yahoo!

People Sources

School or local library personnel. Explain the nature of the business plan and show the librarian the industry, customer, and competitor information that you are to gather and request assistance.

Interviews of people who work in your industry or at a competing firm. The Yellow Pages directory or Web sites will have telephone numbers of companies. Contact them on the telephone or by personal visit. (Industry, customer, and competitor analysis)

Small Business Development Center personnel. This is a division of the Small Business Administration (SBA). An SBA Center office should be in your town or city. Look in the business section of the telephone directory for the listing. (Industry, customer, and competitor analysis)

Chamber of Commerce personnel. This will have statistics on the local population and economy. To contact the chamber office in your town or city, look in the business section of the telephone directory for the listing. (Industry, customer, and competitor analysis)

Miscellaneous Sources

- Visit a competitor. A lot can be learned by asking questions and making observations. This is especially useful if your business is a retail store, restaurant, or service that is visited by customers. (Competitor analysis)
- Look at a brochure or catalog of a firm. (Competitor analysis)
- Read the annual financial report of a firm if a firm's stock is traded on a stock exchange. (Competitor analysis)
- Get a copy of the menu of a restaurant if your business is a restaurant. (Competitor analysis)

When you find information that may be included in the business plan, record the source. All information that is used must be properly cited in the bibliography section at the end of the plan.

Market Segmentation

The needs and wants of people that purchase in most industries are typically very diverse. A company cannot successfully compete if it markets a product or service that is intended to appeal to all customer needs. Companies use a process called *market segmentation* to overcome this problem. It involves grouping prospective customers by similar characteristics they possess. One subgroup of potential customers is selected to be the target of a firm's activities.

There are three common ways of describing potential customers. They involve using demographic, geographic, and psychographic characteristics. *Demographic characteristics* are age, gender, household size, education, occupation, and household income. This is a very popular way of describing a group of potential customers because U.S. Census data is available for analysis. Describing customers based on their location, such as region of the United States, state, local area, or population density (rural, suburban, or urban areas), involves using *geographic characteristics*. If customers have to travel to the business if climate is a consideration, or if consumer needs vary by area, this means of description is useful. *Psychographic characteristics* are another popular means of describing customers. It calls for using interests and lifestyles of people.

Defining a Target Market

A *target market* is the group of customers for which a firm's products or services, pricing, distribution, and promotion are designed. Defining the target market involves describing intended customers using the relevant characteristics that were outlined in the previous section. AVID SPORTS plans to market a high-performance running shoe. The intended target market for the product is described in Exhibit 1.3.

Perceptions and Needs of the Target Market

Once target market customers have been identified, market research must be conducted with them to determine perceptions of the business concept. This data will indicate the potential success of the business concept in the marketplace. Specific needs of target customers must also be

Exhibit 1.3. Target Market for AVID SPORTS Running Shoe

Demographic Characteristics

Age: 25–54
Gender: Male or female
Household size: Varies
Education: College degree
Occupation: Business, legal, or medical professional
Household income: $80,000+

Geographic Characteristics

Region: Entire United States
Population density: Urban or suburban

Psychographic Characteristics

Interests: Nutrition and health; very serious about running
Lifestyle: Very active in sports; runs 15+ miles per week

determined. *Needs* are things that are desired by customers. Respondents who participate in the survey should also be asked to prioritize their needs so that the firm knows which ones are most important. These needs will provide valuable insight regarding product or service design, pricing, and distribution considerations. They also indicate what should be conveyed in advertising.

The questionnaire that AVID used to determine the perceptions and needs of its target market is in Exhibit 1.4.

The results of AVID's survey were very positive. An analysis of the responses produced the findings in Exhibit 1.5.

Exhibit 1.4. Questionnaire for AVID SPORTS Survey

AVID SPORTS

Market Research Questionnaire

AVID SPORTS is a company that is being formed to produce and market the following product:

> A high-performance athletic shoe that has a carbon-fiber plate in the sole that propels a runner into the next stride. It also features a silicone-filled pad in the heel so that shocks from running are absorbed in the shoe.

Considering other running shoes on the market, please rate the proposed shoe on the following criteria:

Uniqueness

Very unique   Not at all
                                                                                              unique

| 1 | 2 | 3 | 4 | 5 |

Desirability of the Features

Very desirable   Not at all
                                                                                            desirable

| 1 | 2 | 3 | 4 | 5 |

In the space below, please list five needs you have for running shoes that you purchase.

Prioritize each of the five needs above by placing "1" next to the most important need, "2" for the next most important need, and so on.

Name _____

Age _____

Gender: Male or female (Please circle)

Highest education level achieved _____

Occupation _____

Average number of days you run per week _____

Average number of miles you run per week _____

Exhibit 1.5. AVID's Survey Findings

Uniqueness of the concept: 1.35 (1 = very unique; 5 = not at all unique)

Desirability of the concept: 1.42 (1 = very desirable; 5 = not at all desirable)

Prioritized needs related to running shoe purchases (1 = most important):

1. Enjoy running more
2. Improve running performance
3. Reduce foot, ankle, and knee injuries
4. Comfort
5. Contemporary styling and design

Demographic information of respondents:

- *Average age*: 36.5 years
- *Gender*: 43.2% Female, 56.8% Male
- *Education level*: 3.5% no college, 30.2% some college, 66.3% college degree
- *Occupation*: 87.2% professional, 12.8% nonprofessional
- *Running*: 3.4 days per week, 16.6 miles per week

Preparing for Team Meetings

If you are working on a team with other students, you should meet as a group to discuss issues related to each section of the plan. Your instructor may ask team members to evaluate the contribution you make to the completion of each section, so thorough preparation for all meetings is essential. The following are the steps you should follow to prepare for team meetings for each section of the business plan.

1. Read and study the chapter that concerns the section of the plan under consideration.
2. Formulate your ideas and recommendations for *all* issues at the end of the chapter. Address all issues in detail.

3. Record your ideas and recommendations. Confirm with your instructor the number of word-processed pages that are required. Be sure to label each issue with the heading in the list of issues. Keep a copy of your written work for future reference.

4. Attend the team meeting and actively participate. At the conclusion of meeting, your instructor may have you give a copy of your written report to a team member who is designated as the "reporting team member" for that section of the business plan.

Concepts to Know

competitor analysis

customer analysis

demographic characteristics

direct competitor

focus group

geographic characteristics

indirect competitor

industry analysis

mail survey

market research

market segmentation

needs

opportunity analysis

personal interview

primary data

psychographic characteristics

questionnaire

secondary data

target market

Chapter 1 Issues: Opportunity Analysis

1. *Preparing for Team Meetings.* If you are a member of a team, refer to the previous section, "Preparing for Team Meetings." Follow the instructions on how to prepare for the meeting concerning the issues that follow.

2. *Industry and Customer Analysis.* Study this chapter. Identify, with assistance from your instructor, the industry in which you will compete. Complete an industry and customer analysis for your business concept. Record bibliographic information for each source that may be cited in your report.

3. *Competitor Analysis.* Complete a competitor profile and analysis of strengths and weaknesses. Consider indirect competitors if direct

competitors do not exist. Ask your instructor how many competitors must be profiled. Record bibliographic information for each
source.

4. *Target Market.* Define the intended target market for your business
   concept using relevant demographic, geographic, and psychographic
   characteristics. Consider the format in Exhibit 1.3.

5. *Target Market Perceptions and Needs.* Create a questionnaire that will
   determine the perceptions, needs, and demographic information of
   your target market. Consider the format in Exhibit 1.4. At the top
   of the form include the business concept statement that you developed in the previous chapter. Conduct this survey with people who
   fit the description of your target market. This can be done in person
   or on the telephone. Ask each respondent to prioritize his or her
   needs (1 = most important). Analyze the data from the completed
   questionnaires and make recommendations on the findings. Consider the format in Exhibit 1.5.

CHAPTER 2

Organization Plan

Looking Ahead

Upon completion of this chapter, you should be able to

1. explain the purpose of the organization plan,
2. identify the name for a company and choose an appropriate form of ownership,
3. determine staffing needs and employee compensation for a new business,
4. design an organizational chart, and
5. choose a location for a new business and design a floor plan.

Purpose of the Organization Plan

The *organization plan* section of the business plan describes how a new firm will be structured and staffed, where it will be located, and what is the office or retail space that it will occupy. This chapter explains how to formulate your plans in the following areas:

- Company Name and Vision
- Forms of Ownership
- Days and Hours of Operation
- Outsourcing
- Staffing and Management Team
- Organizational Chart
- Employee Compensation
- Choosing a Location
- Space Requirements and Leasing

- Equipment, Leased-Space Improvements and Web Site Costs
- Leasing Versus Purchasing Equipment
- Floor Plan

Company Name and Vision

All companies must have a name. An effective name is an important form of promotion that works for the firm 365 days of the year. It helps people recognize businesses and know which ones to patronize. If a firm does a good job serving the needs of customers, *company or brand loyalty* is created and future sales from customers can be anticipated. Establishing the name in people's minds also paves the way for future expansion.

Choosing a name for a business is very important because it can create a sustainable competitive advantage. Ideally the name exhibits these characteristics:

- Easy to remember and pronounce
- Unique versus competitor names
- Presents a positive image for the firm
- Communicates something about the current and future nature of the company
- Designed to be visually distinctive including a unique font or graphic element
- Available for a trademark or service mark

A company name that has no meaning or relevance to the firm's offerings should be avoided. It should be one where the exclusive rights to use the name can be secured. The U.S. Bureau of Patents and Trademarks can grant a *trademark* (TM) for the name of a firm that is not a service. Trademarks can be secured for names of individual products, as well. The bureau can also grant a *service market* (SM) to service firms. Trade and service marks have legal protection and keep competitors from using a name. Ideally, the company name is available as a World Wide Web domain name.

A producer of products should make a distinction between the name of the firm and brand name(s) of individual products. They should not be the same. The company name for a producer must allow for the addition of new products that may not be related to the product that was launched when the business began operations. Brand names for individual products will be addressed in chapter 3 of this book.

In addition to a name, a company should have a stated goal of where it plans to be in the future. A *vision statement* describes this goal and paints a vivid picture of the dream for the company. It considers the future size of the firm, types of products it will offer, and the nature of the customers it will serve. The vision statement provides a path for future growth. It should be only one or two sentences in length.

The first product that the founders in the continuing case will launch is an athletic shoe. The name they have chosen for the company is "AVID SPORTS." The word "avid" was chosen because it means "fondness for." People who are avid about something are enthusiastic about it and pursue it vigorously. "AVID SPORTS" is consistent with the target market for the athletic shoe that will be marketed initially because these people are avid runners. "Sports" was chosen because it is general enough so products that are not athletic shoes can be offered in the future. They have formulated the following vision statement for the company:

> *AVID SPORTS will be a global marketer of high-performance sporting goods for people who are very enthusiastic and knowledgeable about their sport.*

All future products that the company offers will reflect this vision.

Forms of Ownership

Your business must operate within one of three ownership structures: sole proprietorship, partnership, or corporation. A business that is owned by one person is a *sole proprietorship*. A *partnership* is a business owned by two or more people. *Corporations* are firms that have been granted some of the same legal rights as a person by a state government and may have several owners.

Sole proprietorships are by far the most common form of ownership. The owner must secure a license from the city in which the firm is located. This type of business is easy to form and often does not require the assistance of an attorney. The owner enjoys all profits that may be realized; however, she or he is also liable for any debts or legal claims against the business. Financing to launch and operate the business is limited to the resources of the owner or personal loans. Stock cannot be issued to raise capital.

A partnership is very similar to a sole proprietorship except there is more than one owner. The rights and responsibilities of the partners are described in a legal contract called a *partnership agreement*. An attorney is needed to construct the agreement. The advantages and disadvantages to this form of ownership are similar to a sole proprietorship.

Many firms chose the corporate form of ownership. One reason is that the owners have *limited liability*. This means that if the firm goes bankrupt or is involved in litigation, the owners (*stockholders*) are not held liable. The most they can lose is the amount invested in the corporation. Another major reason for incorporating is that the firm may get more financing than other forms of ownership. Corporations can not only secure loans like sole proprietorships and partnerships but also sell stock to raise funds. The major disadvantage to incorporating is *double taxation*; the company's profit and the dividends received by stockholders are both taxed. Another disadvantage to incorporating is an increase in government regulations and paperwork.

Stock represents ownership in the corporation held by stockholders. When a corporation is formed, an arbitrary number of shares of stock are authorized. Some of these shares may be sold to the founders or key managers of the company or people not associated with the firm but who wish to invest. Profits that a corporation realizes can be distributed to shareholders in the form of *stock dividends* or retained in the business for future expansion. Start-up firms typically do not register with a stock exchange and do not publicly sell stock through the exchange. Stock is sold privately to individuals.

As you will see in chapter 4 of the business plan, the funding needed to start your business may be substantial. If your business is a corporation, you will have the opportunity to raise start-up capital through the sale of stock.

AVID has chosen the corporate form of ownership. Its complete name is AVID SPORTS, INC. "Inc." must be included on the firm's letterhead stationary and legal documents to inform people it is a corporation.

Days and Hours of Operation

The days of the week and hours of the day a firm is open for business is determined in part by the needs of customers. Hours of operation of competitors are a consideration for retail stores, restaurants, and service firms that are visited by customers. Costs are also a factor. The more hours you are open, the higher employee compensation will be. Also, extended hours present problems with staffing a business during times when employees do not want to work.

The hours of operation for AVID are 8:30 a.m. to 5:00 p.m., Monday through Friday. These hours are adequate, since AVID is a producer and its customers do not make in-person visits to the firm.

Outsourcing

Many companies have adopted the policy that if a task needs to be performed and it can be done more effectively, efficiently, or at a lower cost by another firm, it should be outsourced. *Outsourcing* is contracting with these firms and having them perform tasks. Some companies have outsourced almost all functions and have very few employees. These are called *virtual companies*. Often functions, tasks, or projects are not ongoing, so hiring permanent employees to perform them would not be cost effective.

Outsourcing to professional advisors is very common. The following are some of the professional advisors that companies use:

- Attorneys who write legal contracts
- Accountants who prepare financial statements and government forms
- Bookkeepers who record sales and expenses, pay bills, and do payroll

- Consultants who provide insight regarding marketing, management, financial planning, and computer technology
- Engineers who design new or improve existing products
- Advertising agencies that create ads and brochures and schedule media

These advisors are *independent contractors*, which mean that they are not employees. The firm contracting with them pays for services on an hourly basis. A highly experienced advisor can cost a firm $150 to $300 per hour.

Functions that are performed on a continuous, daily basis can also be outsourced. A company that is involved in the production of a product can outsource manufacturing. The manufacturer is required to adhere to certain quality standards. Start-up businesses often outsource production because they do not have the resources to lease space or purchase machines for production. If your firm is a producer, planning to outsource manufacturing may be a viable option.

Producers can also outsource warehousing and shipping functions. *Public warehouses* exist in most cities. They lease space to companies. Some will prepare products for shipment and deliver them to customers. Consider outsourcing warehousing and shipping if your business is a producer.

Another function that is often outsourced is selling. Outside sales representatives travel to customers to sell products or services. The cost to employ a full-time representative can be $80,000 to $100,000 per year including compensation, sales administration, a company auto, an expense account, and fringe benefits. If a firm sells its products throughout the country, it might require 40 or more salespeople. The cost for 40 outside salespeople would be $3,200,000 to $4,000,000 a year. Most start-up firms cannot afford this fixed expense so they outsource it.

Firms that offer this service are called *sales agents*. They are independent companies or individuals that perform the selling function for companies in the local market the agent firm or individual serves. A producer offering its products throughout the country would employ several agent firms—one in each major geographic area. Agents do not take ownership or physical possession of products. They meet with customers, write orders, transmit the orders to the producer, and earn a commission of approximately 5% of sales. One final advantage to using agents is that the cost to perform the selling function is variable. It fluctuates with sales. If sales are low, selling expense is also low. If outside salespeople are needed for your business, consider outsourcing the selling function to sales-agent firms or individuals.

AVID plans to outsource several functions. These included manufacturing, warehousing and shipping, selling, product design, and advertising. An attorney and management consultant will also be used when they are needed.

Staffing

There are three functional areas of a business that must be staffed regardless of the type of business: marketing, finance, and operations. The *marketing function* involves planning and executing activities regarding the products or services a firm will offer and how they will be priced, distributed, advertised, and sold. The *finance function* entails accounting, bookkeeping, and securing financing needed to launch and run a business. Managing the day-to-day activities of the business is the *operations function*. Computer information systems are included in the operations function.

A business needs different types of employees. The types of employees required are determined by the skills needed and the tasks that must be performed. To determine the types of employees needed, the entrepreneur begins by listing these skills and tasks. Next, skills and tasks that are related are grouped together to create a position. Finally, a title is assigned to each position and a job description is written. A *job description* is a statement that explains the duties and responsibilities of a position. It includes whether the position is part or full time, the salary or wage rate, and the fringe benefits that will be offered. The qualifications needed to perform the job may also be included.

Management Team

Managers plan, organize, staff, and supervise personnel. The success of a business depends primarily on the skills, knowledge, and abilities of managers that are responsible for the three functional areas described earlier. The number of managers a business needs varies. A medium-sized business, such as a producer of products, may have a manager for each functional area (marketing, finance, and operations). However, a small business that cannot afford a large staff may combine functions and assign them to one person. A small retail store, for example, may have one manager that performs all three functions and also be involved in selling. The only other employees are part-time salespeople. Two managers may be needed in a small restaurant: a general manager that oversees all operations including the waiters and a chef that manages kitchen personnel. The number of managers needed for your business depends on the number of personnel employed, the complexity of operations, and what you can afford. One person can usually manage five to eight full-time employees and more part-time employees.

Organizational Chart

An *organizational chart* illustrates all the positions in a firm and the reporting structure for each position. It clarifies the lines of communication and helps employees know who is in charge of each area. Exhibit 2.1 is and example of the organizational chart for AVID SPORTS.

Stockholders are at the top of the chart in Exhibit 2.1 because they elect the board of directors and the members of the board appoint the president and other corporate officers that are employed by the firm. Corporate officers sometimes have the title of vice president.

AVID's president oversees all operations and reporting to him are the four managers and two professional advisors: an attorney and consultant. The *finance and operations manager* handles the money: sales revenue that comes in and expenses that are paid. The manager also supervises two administrative assistants that work with all employees and is responsible for technology including computers and the telephone system. The *production manager* works closely with a manager at the outsourced manufacturing firm that produces athletic shoes to ensure quality standards

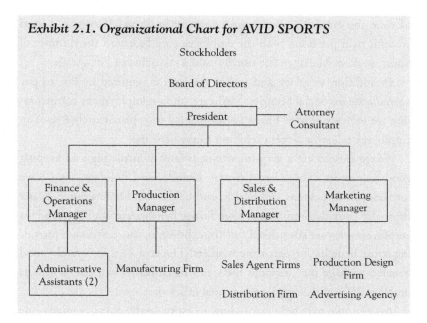

Exhibit 2.1. Organizational Chart for AVID SPORTS

Stockholders

Board of Directors

President — Attorney Consultant

Finance & Operations Manager

Production Manager

Sales & Distribution Manager

Marketing Manager

Administrative Assistants (2)

Manufacturing Firm

Sales Agent Firms

Production Design Firm

Distribution Firm

Advertising Agency

and delivery schedules are met. The *sales manager* works with a manager at each sales-agent firm that performs the selling function in a geographic area. This manager also coordinates shipments to customers through the distribution firm that warehouses and transports products. Product design, pricing, distribution, and promotion are the responsibilities of the *marketing manager*. This person works with an outside firm that employs specialists that design, construct, and test prototypes of new athletic shoes. The marketing manager also works with an advertising agency.

A small firm such as a retail store with one manager who performs all the functions of the business and supervises part-time salespeople does not need an organizational chart.

Employee Compensation

Compensation is not only a means to reward employees for their efforts but also a way to attract and retain the best employees. It can take three forms: salary, wages, and fringe benefits. *Salary* is a fixed amount of compensation that is stated for a 12-month period. Assume a marketing manager earns a salary of $60,000 a year. Salary is not affected by the amount of time the employee spends on company business. A *wage* is a fixed amount paid per hour, with the employee paid based on the number of hours worked. Managers are usually paid a salary instead of a wage.

In addition to salary and wages, the firm is required by law to pay *payroll taxes* for Social Security, Medicare, and unemployment compensation for each employee. This amount is equal to approximately 8% of an employee's salary or wages excluding fringe benefits.

Fringe benefits are a very important means of attracting and keeping good employees. These benefits may include paid holidays, paid leave for vacation or sickness and health, and dental and life insurance. Many firms also provide a retirement plan. Fringe benefits are often reserved for employees who are considered full-time; however, more firms are providing some benefits for part-time workers. The cost of a reasonably good benefits package that includes the items listed earlier can cost a firm as much as 25% of the employee's annual salary or wages.

An example may help clarify how to estimate the cost to employ one person. Assume a full-time manager employed by AVID earns $50,000 per year in salary, and he or she is provided with fringe benefits. The total cost would be the following:

- $50,000 annual salary
- $4,000 payroll taxes (8% of annual salary)
- $12,500 fringe benefits (25% of annual salary)
- $66,500 total compensation cost

Compensation is a major expense for companies. Firms must balance the advantages of a good compensation package with the disadvantage of higher costs.

AVID SPORTS plans on having a president, four managers, and one administrative assistant that are full-time employees and earn an annual salary. They receive fringe benefits as well. One additional administrative assistant will be employed who is paid an hourly wage and who does not receive fringe benefits. AVID must pay payroll taxes for all seven employees. The firm is open from 8:30 a.m. to 5:00 p.m., Monday through Friday throughout the year. The annual cost for compensation for AVID is illustrated in Exhibit 2.2.

Exhibit 2.2. Annual Compensation Expense for AVID SPORTS

Position	Annual salary	Wages/ year	Payroll taxes	Fringe benefits	Total compensation
President	$70,000		$5,600	$17,500	$93,100
Finance/ operations manager	50,000		4,000	12,500	66,500
Production manager	50,000		4,000	12,500	66,500
Sales/ distribution manager	50,000		4,000	12,500	66,500
Marketing manager	50,000		4,000	12,500	66,500
Administrative asst. (full-time)	30,000		2,400	7,500	39,900
Administrative asst. (part-time @ $10/hour 25 hours/week, 50 weeks/year)		$12,500	1,000	0	13,500
Total	$300,000	$12,500	$25,000	$75,000	$412,500

Total Compensation for Year 1 = $412,500

Payroll taxes were calculated at 8% of salary or wages. Fringe benefits were calculated at 25% of salary. The part-time administrative assistant does not receive fringe benefits.

Choosing a Location

Choosing a geographic location for your business is very important, especially if it is a retail store, restaurant, or service that is visited by customers. A poor location can result in failure even if all other aspects of the business are superior.

There are many factors that must be considered in choosing a location that customers will visit. First, the *trading area* is important. This is the geographic area from which you can expect customers to travel. The trading area for a gas station or convenience store may only be 2 miles.

However, people may drive 20 miles to a specialty store, for example, that has little or no competition and sells exclusive imported rugs at discount prices.

Two other factors in choosing a location are the location of potential customers and of existing competitors. The *demographic characteristics* of people (age, gender, income, education, and employment) living in different areas can vary widely. The demographic profile of people in an area should parallel the profile of your target market. Proximity to competitors can be something to avoid or desire. Distance from a competitor is advisable if there is no perceivable difference in your offerings. Being close to a competitor is an asset if people want to do comparative shopping. Furniture stores often locate near one another for this reason.

Additional factors to consider in choosing a location for a business that is visited by customers are access to roads, highways, or public transportation; drive-by or walk-by traffic volume; visibility from the road or walkway; availability of parking; exterior lighting; crime levels; and the surrounding neighborhood.

Once a geographic location is chosen, the type of building must be considered. A retail store, restaurant, or service that is visited by customers can be located in a stand-alone building, strip mall, or major shopping mall. Advantages to a *stand-alone building* are that the design of the building exterior can be made to reinforce the image of the firm, and there are often fewer operational restrictions imposed by the landlord. There is also the possibility of purchasing the building in the future. The advantage to locating in a *strip mall* or *major shopping mall* is that people who shop at another business in the mall may also visit your store.

Location is not as critical for businesses that produce a product or offer a service but are not visited by customers. However, access to customers, suppliers, and roadways may be important. Zoning laws and crime in an area are also considerations. These firms normally lease space in an existing building.

Space Requirements and Leasing

Most start-up firms do not have the resources to purchase a building. They *lease space* from a landlord. You may wish to consider leasing the space that your company will occupy.

Office, retail, and restaurant space is leased based on the square footage needed. Square footage is calculated by multiplying the length of the interior space times the width. A space with dimensions of 40 feet by 25 feet is 1,000 square feet.

To estimate the space needed for your business, identify a company that is similar to the one you have in mind. If your concept is a retail store or restaurant, call or visit the firm and ask the manager the size of the space that they occupy. The following information will help you determine the space needed for your business.

A fully equipped office should have 100 square feet for each employee workstation plus an additional 50 square feet per employee to provide space for a reception area; an employee lounge/conference area; and equipment such as a copier, hallways, and storage. Small offices in an office building typically use restrooms that are available to all employees that work in the building. Large offices have their own restrooms.

Retail Store

Size of store	Merchandise & cashier area (sq. ft.)	Storage area (sq. ft.)	Office & lounge area (sq. ft.)	Total leased space (sq. ft.)
Small*	1,020	180	—	1,200
Midsize	2,550	350	100	3,000
Large	8,500	1,100	400	10,000

*Small retail stores do not have an office or employee lounge area.

Restaurant

Size of restaurant	Dining tables	Seats (4/ table)	Dining & cashier area (sq. ft.)	Kitchen & storage, etc. (sq. ft.)	Total leased space (sq. ft.)
Small	20	80	1,700	700	2,400
Midsize	40	160	3,400	1,400	4,800
Large	60	240	5,100	2,100	7,200

An average-sized dining table in a restaurant has four seats. The area noted in the table for the kitchen and storage includes space for restrooms. A large restaurant would also have an office and employee lounge in the space noted in the table.

The cost per square foot to lease space for 1 year varies depending on the type of space. Costs are high for retail stores and restaurants because high-traffic locations are needed. Warehouse space is the least expensive. The following are some average costs to lease space that will be helpful in calculating your annual lease expense. These do not include the cost for utilities. Costs to lease space in major cities such as Chicago or Los Angeles can be two to three times higher than indicated. The minimum duration of a lease is generally 3 years.

Office space for a producer	$16 per square foot per year or service firm
Warehouse space	$6 per square foot
Retail store space	$35 per square foot
Restaurant space	$25 per square foot

An example will help illustrate how to calculate your lease expense for a 12-month period. AVID SPORTS is planning to lease office space in an industrial park for its seven employees. The interior dimensions of the space will be 40 feet by 25 feet. This office is 1,000 square feet (40 feet times 25 feet). Seven hundred square feet are needed for employee work-stations and 300 square feet will be used for a reception area, employee lounge/conference area, and storage. At $16 per square foot, the annual lease expense will be $16,000 (1,000 feet times $16 per foot). Warehouse space is not needed to store athletic shoes and prepare them for shipment because AVID will outsource these functions.

Lease payments do not include the cost to initially remodel the space or equip it. These are discussed in the following section. Costs for staff and other operating expenses are excluded as well.

Equipment, Leased-Space Improvements, and Web Site Costs

Once space has been secured it must be remodeled and equipped for operations. The following is a list of some items that are needed to start a business. Estimated costs are also provided. The nature of your business will determine which items are appropriate.

One of the costs provided below is for an e-commerce Web site. This type of site can accept orders and payments from customers. The cost for an e-commerce site is very high. You may decide not to have this type of Web site in the first year unless your firm is a Web-based business. A site that provides only promotional information may still be a consideration. This will be discussed in chapter 3.

Office

- Fully equipped and installed employee workstation including divider panels, desk, chair, file cabinet, and lighting: $2,500 per station
- Employee lounge/conference area equipment—coffeemaker, microwave, refrigerator, one table, and six chairs: $2,000
- Cash register, exterior signage, and technology (see "Other Equipment")
- Leased-space improvements: $0 to $50 per square foot for remodeling. (The amount depends on the condition of the initial space and the design of the new space.)

Retail Store

- Display fixtures and shelving: $6 per square foot of the area where merchandise is displayed. (If the merchandise display area is 1,000 square feet, $6,000 will be needed for these fixtures.)
- Office (see above)
- Employee lounge (for large stores only; see "Office")
- Cash register, exterior signage, and technology (see "Other Equipment")
- Leased-space improvements: $40 to $125 per square foot for remodeling. (The amount depends on the condition of the initial space and the design of the new space.)

Restaurant

- Kitchen equipment: $100,000 to $300,000 depending on size of kitchen
- Construction of a bar and bar equipment (if required): $50,000

- One dining table and 4 chairs: $1,000 per set
- Plates, cups, glassware, silverware, and initial supplies: $300 per table
- Office (see "Office" entry)
- Employee lounge (for large restaurants only; see "Office")
- Cash register, exterior signage, and technology (see "Other Equipment")
- Leased-space improvements for remodeling (same as for a retail store)

Warehouse

- Shelving or pallet racks: $4,000 per 1,000 square feet of warehouse space
- Used lift truck (if required): $5,000
- Shipping area equipment: $2,000
- Start-up shipping cartons and supplies: $3,000

Other Equipment (If Required)

- Delivery vehicle: Depends on the size and type of vehicle. Contact local dealers that sell used or new vehicles.
- Cash register: $1,000 each (no scanner); $5,000 each (with scanner)
- Exterior sign mounted on the storefront: $4,000 (3 feet by 8 feet, illuminated, and installed)
- Exterior sign mounted on a pole by the roadway: $10,000 (6 feet by 6 feet, illuminated and installed)
- Technology
  - Computer with software: $1,500 each
  - Networking several computers so that they can all access a central database (installed): $3,000 plus the cost of each computer
  - Computer printer (commercial grade): $1,500 each
  - Fax machine (commercial grade): $1,000 each
  - Photocopy machine (commercial grade): $1,000 each
  - Telephone (installed): $200 each

- Telephone system with voicemail in which several telephones are connected (installed): $4,000 excluding the cost of telephones
- Specialized equipment: This depends on the nature of the business. (For example, a lawn care business needs mowers, leaf blowers, trucks, and trailers.)

E-commerce Web Site (Web-Based Businesses Only)

- Initial Web site development: $50,000 to $200,000

Exhibit 2.3 indicates the equipment and leased-space improvement costs for AVID SPORTS. The company will have seven employees.

Exhibit 2.3. Equipment, Leased-Space Improvements, and Web Site Costs for AVID SPORTS

	Costs
Equipment and Vehicles:	
Fully equipped employee workstations—7 stations @ $2,500 per station	$17,500
Employee lounge equipment—1 @ $2,000	2,000
Warehouse equipment and delivery vehicle—none, because AVID is outsourcing warehousing and delivery of products to customers	0
Exterior signage—none, because customers do not visit the firm	0
Technology	
Computer with software—7 @ $1,500 each	10,500
Networking computers	3,000
Computer printer—2 @ $1,500 each	3,000
Fax machine—1 @ $1,000	1,000
Photocopy machine—1 @ $1,000	1,000
Telephones—7 @ $200 each	1,400
Telephone system with voicemail	4,000
Cost for equipment and vehicles	$ 43,400
Leased-Space Improvements:	
No remodeling is needed because the office space that will be leased is in move-in condition.	$ 0
E-commerce Web Site:	
None in Year 1. AVID's site will be for promotion only not e-commerce.	$ 0

Leasing Versus Purchasing Equipment

As you can see from the list in Exhibit 2.3, the start-up costs for a business are substantial. Owners of new businesses often do not have sufficient funds to purchase all that is needed to begin operations. There are firms that work with business owners to lease equipment until the cost of items is paid.

Floor Plan

Once you have determined the number of employees, the equipment and technology needed, and the size of the space required for your business, a floor plan of the business can be developed. A *floor plan* indicates where everything is going to be located in the space. This may include a reception area, employee workstations, furniture, equipment, employee lounge/conference area, bathrooms, storage area, doorways, and aisles. The floor plan for a retail store indicates shelving and tables to display merchandise as well as a cashier's area. A clothing store needs a dressing room. A restaurant floor plan includes where each table is to be located as well as the area for the cashier, kitchen, restrooms, storage, and an office, if required. Any type of business that customers visit must consider traffic flow in the space. Refer to the previous section, "Space Requirements and Leasing," for other considerations. Floor plans are drawn to scale, ideally on graph paper where a unit of space on the plan is equal to 1 foot. Exhibit 2.4 is a floor plan for AVID's office that will have seven employees.

Exhibit 2.4. Floor Plan for AVID SPORTS

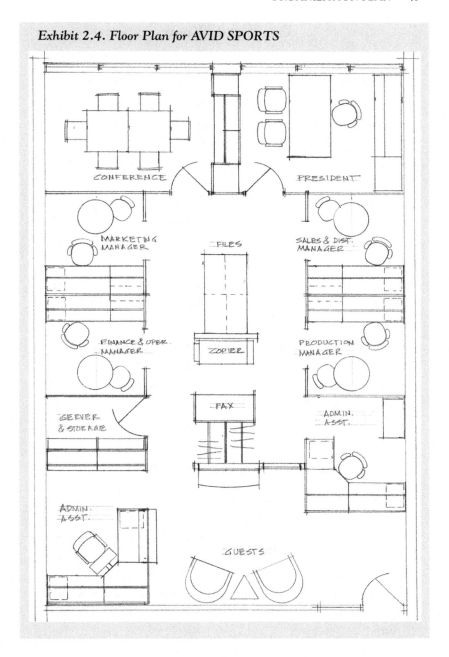

Concepts to Know

company or brand loyalty	partnership
compensation	partnership agreement
corporation	payroll taxes
demographic characteristics	president
finance and operations manager	production manager
finance function	public warehouse
floor plan	salary
fringe benefits	sales agent
independent contractor	sales manager
job description	service mark (SM)
leased space	sole proprietorship
limited liability of a corporation	stock
manager	stock dividends
marketing function	stockholder
marketing manager	trademark
operations function	trading area
organizational chart	virtual company
organizational plan	vision statement
outsourcing	wage

Chapter 2 Issues: Organization Plan

1. *Preparing for Team Meetings.* If you are a member of a team, refer to the section "Preparing for Team Meetings" in chapter 1. Follow the instructions on preparing for the meeting concerning the issues that follow.

2. *Company Name and Vision.* Study this chapter. Identify potential names for your company. Select the best name and explain why it was chosen. Write a one- or two-sentence vision statement for your firm.

3. *Form of Ownership.* Determine the form of ownership. Explain the benefits for this form of ownership.

4. *Outsourcing.* Is outsourcing advisable for your firm? If so, what areas will be outsourced?

5. *Days and Hours of Operation.* What days and hours will your firm be open for business?

6. *Staffing and Management Team.* Determine the type and number of nonmanagerial employees that are needed for your business. Assign each job a title. Determine how many managers your firm needs. What functional areas will they manage and what are their titles?

7. *Organizational Chart.* Construct an organizational chart for your business that indicates all positions. Consider the format in Exhibit 2.1.

8. *Employee Compensation.* Consider the number of hours each employee will work during the first 12 months of operations. Calculate total employee compensation expense including salary, wages, payroll taxes, and fringe benefits. Consider the format in Exhibit 2.2.

9. *Location.* Recommend a specific geographic location for your business. If your concept is a retail store, restaurant, or service that is visited by customers, consider the trading area and whether it will be in a stand-alone building, strip mall, or major shopping mall. For all concepts, describe why this location is desirable.

10. *Equipment, Leased-Space Improvements, and Web Site.* Make a list of the furniture, equipment, fixtures, vehicles, and technology needed to start your business. Include the number of units required, cost per unit, and total cost for each item. Estimate the cost to remodel the space you will be leasing. If your company is a Web-based business, estimate the cost for Web site development. What will be the total cost for all of these items? Consider the format in Exhibit 2.3.

11. *Space Requirements.* Calculate the total square footage needed for your business and estimate the annual cost to lease space.

12. *Floor Plan.* Design a floor plan (to scale) of the space you will be leasing. Consider the format in Exhibit 2.4.

CHAPTER 3

Marketing Plan

Looking Ahead

Upon completion of this chapter, you should be able to

1. explain the purpose of the marketing plan;
2. develop product, service, pricing, distribution, and promotion strategies for a business;
3. create selling, advertising, publicity, and sales promotion programs;
4. recommend strategies that will provide future growth for a business; and
5. forecast sales revenue.

Purpose of the Marketing Plan

Many people have a misconception of the term "marketing." They often think it means "advertising," "promotion," or "retailing." It includes these, but it is much broader in scope. *Marketing* is anything that is designed to bring buyers and sellers together.

There are four elements that facilitate buyer-seller exchanges: a *product (or service)* that is unique and desired by buyers, a *price* for the product that buyers feel offers good value, a means of *distribution* so that buyers can gain access to the product, and *promotion* to make buyers aware of the product and its unique benefits. Chapter 2 describes these four elements in detail. This chapter will explain how to determine your plans in the following areas.

- Product or Service Strategy
- Pricing Strategy
- Distribution Strategy

- Forms of Promotion
- Selling Strategy
- Advertising Strategy
- Publicity Strategy
- Sales Promotion Strategy
- Future Growth Strategies
- Sales Forecast

Product or Service Strategy

Product or service strategy is a detailed description of what will be sold to customers. It includes the brand name and packaging if the concept is a product that is being produced. If the concept is a service that will be visited by customers, a retail store, or a restaurant, interior store atmospherics and exterior store appearance must also be considered.

There are two major conditions that must exist for a product, service, or store to be successful in the marketplace. First, it must be unique. This means that very few or no competitors offer the same features or the competitors' features are low in quality. Second, the features must be highly desirable by the target market.

The ideal process to determine these features was used when you completed your opportunity analysis in chapter 1. Recall the needs that you identified for your desired customers. These needs will indicate one or two important features your product or service should offer.

In chapter 2 you identified a name for your company. Firms that produce products must also have names for individual products. These are called *brand names*. The characteristics of a good brand name are the same as for a company name. If you are to identify a brand name, review the section titled "Company Name and Vision" in chapter 2 for a list of these characteristics.

The founders of AVID SPORTS chose "Propell" as the brand name for its first product, a high-performance athletic shoe that is designed for serious runners. There are several reasons why this is an effective name. First, it says something about the product. The shoe has a carbon-fiber plate in the sole that *propels* the runner into the next stride, like a pole-vaulter's pole that propels an athlete over the bar. The extra "L" in the name makes it distinctive. Propell is simple, easy to remember and pronounce, and unique versus competitor names. Products that are launched in the future that offer the propulsion feature may use the same name. Other products will require different brand names.

If your concept is a product that will be produced, packaging is another consideration. *Packaging* performs many functions including containing, storing, protecting, and dispensing the product. A well-designed package and label can serve as an effective means of promotion. Color, graphics, size, and shape can make the product stand out on store shelves. The package can also reinforce the image and brand name of the product. Designing a package that is friendly to the environment should always be an important consideration.

If your concept is a service that is visited by customers, a retail store, or a restaurant, store atmospherics and exterior store appearance must be considered. *Atmospherics* is the general appearance of the store interior including layout, type of fixtures (shelving and displays or tables and chairs), width of aisles, height of the ceiling, lighting, décor, signage, music, and clothes that employees wear. The appearance can greatly enhance the shopping or dining experience. *Exterior store appearance* including signage is very important because it is also like an ad for the store. It must catch the attention of people and be inviting. Atmospherics and store exterior should be unique versus competitors and reinforce the desired image. Visits to competitor firms will reveal their atmospherics and exterior store appearance.

Pricing Strategy

Pricing strategy involves determining the initial price level of what is sold. If the price is too high, sales will be lost. A price that is lower than it needs to be means that profits will be lost. There are five factors that will help determine the initial price:

1. Costs (product or service and operational costs)
2. Price elasticity (sensitivity of customers to different price levels)
3. Desired image
4. Value that the product, service, or store offers
5. Price levels of competitors

The marketing manager can use a number of ways to determine a price. A simple means is to consider three pricing options: penetration, parity, and skimming pricing strategies. A *penetration pricing strategy* is introducing a new product or service at a price below its value but not its costs. This is often below competitor price points. The advantage of this strategy is that high initial sales will be realized. The disadvantage, of course, is that initial profits are lower. *Parity pricing strategy* is pricing a new product at or near competitor levels. This is not likely to result in a pricing response from competitors. However, parity pricing means that price will not create a competitive advantage. A *skimming pricing strategy* is the opposite of a penetration pricing strategy. The product is introduced at levels above its value. This strategy enables the firm to recoup development costs early and create a prestige image. Sales may be limited, however, if there are competitors with lower prices or customers cannot afford the product.

The price for a producer's product that is sold in retail stores must consider the retailer's markup. The pricing of Propell, AVID's high-performance running shoe, can serve as an example. AVID has chosen a skimming pricing strategy because the shoe offers an important benefit that is not available in other athletic shoes. The competitor analysis completed in chapter 1 indicated that the retail price of comparable competitor shoes is $150. The marketing manager has decided that $179 should be the suggested retail price per pair for Propell running shoes. Many retailers use a 100% markup on their cost to determine the retail price. In other words, they take the price that is charged by the producer and double it. The price AVID must charge the retailer that will result in a retail price of $179 is $89.50 per pair ($89.50 + $89.50 = $179). Sales revenue that AVID realizes will be $89.50 per pair of shoes that are sold to the retailer—not $179 per pair.

The price of a pure service is often quoted based on a cost per hour for services rendered. The price per hour includes the total compensation to the employee providing the service plus an additional amount to cover all other costs of doing business and produce a profit. Retail stores and restaurants must price each individual item. A helpful tool for these firms is to estimate the average sale for each customer served. The average sale to one customer purchasing in a gift store, for example, could be $20. A family restaurant might estimate that the average sale for a luncheon meal including a beverage would be $10 per customer served. A dinner meal could be $15. The averages for fast food restaurants would be less while it would be considerably more for fine-dining restaurants. Menus from competitors will indicate their pricing levels.

Distribution Strategy

Distribution strategy concerns making products or services available when and where the target market wants them. "When" has to do with months of the year, weeks of a month, days of the week, and time of the day. Some businesses are open 24 hours per day, 365 days a year. For example, banks make cash available anytime with automated teller machines (ATMs) and e-commerce Web sites allow firms to sell their products at all times of the day. Most firms have limited times when they are open. "Where" concerns the specific geographic location and number of locations where products or services can be purchased. E-commerce and catalogs provide an opportunity for customers to purchase from their homes.

Products and services must be accessible to consumers. The route that products and services take from producer to consumer is called a *channel of distribution*. Exhibit 3.1 illustrates four channels of distribution. *Suppliers* ship raw materials or component parts to producers. *Producers* manufacture finished products. Service firms are also considered producers. Producers may decide to sell directly to consumers. This is illustrated in Exhibit 3.1 as channel A. A producer of swimming pool chemicals that has a Web site and is involved in e-commerce is using a *direct channel* because there are no intermediaries between the producer and consumer. H&R Block tax service also uses this channel since it produces a tax service and sells directly to consumers.

Many producers of tangible products find that it is more efficient to use agents, wholesalers, or retailers to distribute products. This is called an *indirect channel of distribution* because one or more independent firms are between the producer and consumers. Channels B, C, and D in Exhibit 3.1 are examples. A soft drink bottler that delivers directly to supermarkets is using channel B. Kellogg uses channel C when shipping

Exhibit 3.1. Channels of Distribution for Consumer Products

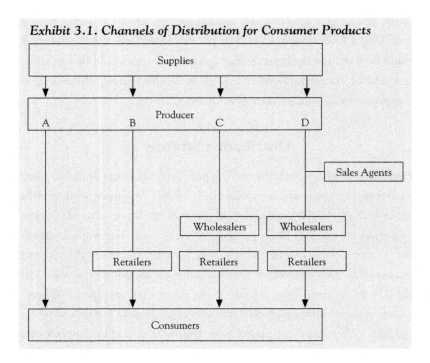

a truckload of breakfast cereal to a wholesaler. The wholesaler ships cases of cereal to retail supermarkets.

Producers sometimes use *sales agents*. These are independent firms that represent the producer and perform the selling function for the producer. This is illustrated by channel D in the Exhibit 3.1. Sales agents do not take physical possession or ownership of products. They are restricted to sell in a specified geographic area and are paid a commission of approximately 5% of sales. A producer that is offering its products in a large area contracts with several sales agents—one for each geographic region. Small, start-up firms that want widespread distribution often use sales agents because they can't afford to employ their own sales representatives. Compensating agents only when sales are realized means that if sales are low, sales expense is low.

A producer may use only one channel of distribution; however, large, established companies may use several channels. *Multiple channels* are desirable because greater access to consumers can be achieved. Pepsi uses many channels: supermarkets, bars, restaurants, vending machines, and so on.

Producers that gain access to consumers through retail stores must decide on the types of outlets that are desired as well as the number of outlets. *Intensive distribution* is where the producer wants to be present in as many stores as possible in an area. Greater access to consumers should result in higher sales. *Selective distribution* calls for only two or three high-quality outlets in an area. Sometimes it is best to have only one retailer in an area. This is called *exclusive distribution*. The advantage to this strategy is that the chosen retailer is more likely to aggressively promote the producer's products.

The Internet provides an opportunity for producers to accept orders and payments from customers. A Web site that allows customers to process orders is called *e-commerce*. The cost to create an e-commerce site can be $50,000 to $200,000 and more. Due to the expense involved, consider not having an e-commerce site in Year 1 unless you have a Web-based business.

Companies can have a Web site and not be involved in e-commerce. If the site is used just for promoting products, it is a form of advertising. Start-up firms may begin with a site that only promotes products. The e-commerce features are added to the site after Year 1. This type of site can be a consideration in your plans for promotion, which is discussed later in this chapter.

The marketing manager at AVID SPORTS formulated the distribution strategy for Propell running shoes. It is summarized in Exhibit 3.2.

Exhibit 3.2. Distribution Strategy for Propell Running Shoes

Coverage area: Entire United States; Year 1 goal is to secure distribution in 180 stores

Channel of distribution: AVID SPORTS > sales agents > wholesalers > retailers > consumers

Geographic area coverage: Exclusive distribution (one retailer per market area)

Stores stocking Propell: Sporting-goods specialty stores that cater to serious athletes

E-commerce: None in Year 1

Forms of Promotion

Promotion is any means used to inform, persuade, or remind customers. It is marketing communication that is intended to enhance sales. There are four forms of promotion: selling, advertising, publicity, and sales promotion. Before promotion strategies can be formulated, an understanding of each form is necessary.

Selling is person-to-person promotion. A sales representative delivers the promotional message to a customer. The advantages to this method are that the impact of the message is high because ample time can be spent with customers, and they are more apt to pay attention to the message. The disadvantage is that the cost of each sales call can be very high if sales representatives travel to customers.

Advertising involves using mass media such as television and newspapers to deliver the promotional message. The broadcaster or publication is paid for the ads that are scheduled. The advantages to this method are that the cost to reach each customer is low, and a large audience can be reached. The disadvantage is that there will be numerous ads for other firms in a medium where they compete for the customer's attention.

Publicity is promotion appearing in print or broadcast mass media as part of the news. For example, publicity is being used if a news article appears about a new store that is opening. The advantage to this is that, unlike advertising that is paid for, publicity is free. However, the disadvantage is that scheduling cannot be guaranteed since news directors determine what news stories are scheduled.

Sales promotion is any promotion that is not considered selling, advertising, or publicity. Coupons, sweepstakes, contests, and temporary price reductions are examples. The advantage to these methods is that higher sales can be realized immediately. However, postpromotion sales can be low because customers buy a large quantity of the product during the promotion, creating a disadvantage: They do not need more for some time.

Selling Strategy

Selling is the most important form of promotion for most firms because it can consistently produce more sales than advertising, publicity, or sales promotion. Selling is people-to-people promotion.

There are four types of sales positions: retail sales representatives, customer service representatives, outside sales representatives, and telemarketers. *Retail sales representatives* sell to customers in a retail store. Some restaurants consider waiters to be responsible for selling. Waiters describe the specials for the day and can use suggestive selling techniques to encourage customers to order drinks, appetizers, dessert, and other items.

Producers and service firms often use customer service representatives, outside sales representatives, and/or telemarketers to perform the selling function. *Customer service personnel* accept incoming telephone calls from customers who want to place orders or who need information. *Outside salespeople* travel to customers to make sales presentations.

Outside salespeople can be employees of the firm or the firm can hire independent sales agents to make sales calls. Refer to the discussion on distribution strategy in the previous section for more on sales agents. *Telemarketers* make outgoing telephone calls to prospective customers.

Advertising Strategy

Advertising involves using mass media to deliver a promotional message. The most popular media are the following:

newspapers	outdoor billboards
magazines	radio
direct mail	television
Yellow Pages	Web site

Newspapers offer broad coverage of a specific local area; however, many people who read a newspaper might not be in your target market.

Magazine advertising can be placed in local or national publications. Local magazines offer the advertiser local coverage of an area, while national magazines often target people that have a special interest in a product or service area. Examples of special-interest magazines are *Auto Trend* and *Runner's World*. The high cost to produce color ads is a disadvantage to magazines.

Direct mail offers the advantage of buying mailing lists for specific target markets. For example, a list could be purchased for seniors in high school. All mailings would be sent to this group with little waste. The main disadvantage to direct mail is that the cost to reach a large number of people is high because of the cost of each mailing and the postage to send them.

Ads in the Yellow Pages in telephone directories can be effective because local customers who are considering a purchase refer to the directory just before purchasing. A simple company listing consisting of the firm's name and address is not very expensive; however, depending on the size of the ad, an ad with more details can be very expensive. A listing provides 12 months of exposure because the telephone directory is in circulation for this period.

Outdoor billboards are very inexpensive on a cost-per-person basis, as many people drive by a billboard. The disadvantage to this medium is that many people who see the ad are not in your target market.

Radio can be an efficient way of reaching a target market if the correct station is chosen. But radio does not offer visual communication.

Television advertising can be purchased for a local, regional, or national area. It has high impact because television offers sight, sound, and motion. The cost to produce and buy commercials is a major disadvantage.

Web sites offer the advantage of providing a large amount of promotional information to potential customers throughout the world. One challenge is to get viewers to a site. Banner ads on search engines and other sites with a link to your site can help. Another drawback is the cost to create the site. A company that serves one local market may not need a Web site in Year 1.

Selecting the best media for an advertising campaign involves answering this question: What media will reach my target market with as little waste as possible? Assume, for example, that your target market is women between the ages of 12 and 25. Advertising in newspapers, outdoor billboards, and primetime television would not be advisable because most people who see the ads are not potential customers. Young women's magazines, direct mail, and top-40 radio stations would be better choices.

The budget for advertising varies a great deal among companies. Some do not use advertising, while others spend as much as 30% of sales on advertising. The average advertising budget is 5% of sales revenue. Spending 10% of sales in Year 1 is often necessary to create initial awareness.

Once media have been selected, advertisements must be created. The words in an ad are called *advertising copy*. The *advertising appeals* are the benefits of the product that are communicated in ad copy. They explain why it should be purchased and clearly and concisely state the competitive advantage. The survey that you conducted in chapter 1 reveals benefits that your customers desire. Benefits that were most desirable should be in your ads.

A *slogan* is a short, catchy phrase that reinforces the copy in an ad and repeats the main benefit. Ads in print media and television require one or more graphic elements to get people's attention and reinforce the appeals. The theme, appeals, and slogan in all media should be consistent to provide repetition of the message to customers.

Publicity Strategy

Publicity is promotion appearing in print or broadcast media as part of the news. Coverage of your company or product can appear in local and national media. News directors decide what stories will be featured; therefore, to get publicity you must have something important to say or a story will not run.

The best way to get news coverage is to write a *news release* that explains what you have to offer that is newsworthy and who to contact for more information. The release should be double-spaced and not more that one page in length. It does not provide all the information needed for a story but rather only enough to motivate a reporter to call for details. A fact sheet and photographs can be sent to news directors with the release.

One way to get publicity is to organize or cosponsor a special event that is newsworthy. An example would be organizing a food or clothing drive for the homeless. Another is participating as a cosponsor for Toys for Tots. Ideally, the event relates to the type of products or services you sell.

Sales Promotion Strategy

Any form of promotion that is not considered selling, advertising, or publicity is sales promotion. It can be directed to consumers, retail firms, waiters, and salespeople. Different forms of sales promotion for each are listed on this page.

Sales Promotion for Consumers

- Free samples
- Coupons
- Rebates
- Sweepstakes
- Contests
- Reduced prices during sales
- Brochures with product or service information

Sales Promotion Offered by Producers to Retail Firms

- Discounts for large purchases that result in in-store displays of the product and a reduced price
- Co-op advertising (funds to advertise the producer's product)
- Point-of-purchase signs and banners
- Trade shows sponsored by producers that display or demonstrate products to retailers who attend the show and are seeking new products

Sales Promotion for Waiters, Customer Service Representatives, and Sales Representatives/Agents

- Manual to educate salespeople on the unique features of the product or service
- Training on selling techniques and product knowledge
- Sales contest with prizes to winners
- Sales meetings for motivation and training
- Bonus for achieving a specific level of sales

During the launch of a new consumer product, producers typically use one or two forms of sales promotion for consumers: one for retail firms and one or two forms for sales representatives and agents. Other firms often use one form of consumer sales promotion and one or two forms of sales promotion for salespeople during the launch of a company.

The promotion strategies for the launch of Propell are outlined in Exhibit 3.3.

Future Growth Strategies

Potential investors are not only interested in the nature of your company during the initial launch of the business concept but also in where it will

---

Exhibit 3.3. Promotion Strategies for Propell in Year 1

Selling Strategy

Use independent sales agents—one in each major market area through-out the United States.

Advertising Strategy

Media: Run ads in *Runner's World* and *Running Times*. Also create a Web site with product information and a list of stores that stock Propell. Invest 10% of sales revenue in Year 1 in advertising and sales promotion.

Advertisements: Appeal to the needs of improved running performance and reduced injuries. Explain that the carbon-fiber plate in the sole of the shoe propels the runner forward like a pole vaulter's pole. Also mention that there is a silicone-filled pad in the heel so that shocks from running are absorbed in the shoe. Include a list of stores that stock Propell. The primary visual in the ad will be a close-up photograph of the Propell shoe worn by a runner. The shoe is in mid-stride. A graphic element will be used to convey the propelling feature of the shoe. The slogan on the ad will be *"Propell. Peak Performance."* The ad will direct customers to the promotional Web site for more information about the product and store locations.

Exhibit 3.3. (continued)

Publicity Strategy

Mail a news release to editors of all sports magazines and sports editors of daily newspapers. Explain the unique features of the shoe. Include a color photograph of the shoe and an actual sample of the carbon-fiber propulsion plate. Sponsor one world-class runner who will be competing in the Boston and New York marathons.

Sales Promotion Strategy

To the consumer: Consumers will see the point-of-purchase display card mentioned below.

To the retailer: A point-of-purchase card will be placed in stores that stock Propell. It will briefly describe the unique features of the shoe. Co-op advertising will also be offered to retailers: AVID will reimburse stores 50% of the cost of advertising they schedule in local newspapers and magazines. Our marketing manager will attend three sporting goods trade shows during the year to introduce Propell to store managers in attendance.

To the independent sales agents: A manual will be given to each of our sales representatives. It will contain details about the product and pricing, the overall marketing program for Propell, and techniques on how to convince retailers to stock the product. Five percent commissions will be paid on sales.

be in 3 to 5 years. What products or services will be offered? What geographic area will be served? How large will the firm be in the future? The four most common means of providing future growth for a business are differentiation, new product or service development, market expansion, and franchising.

Differentiation is improving an existing product or service to make it superior to competition. Advertising often conveys that a product is "new and improved." Differentiation can be achieved for products by adding new features, updating design, and improving quality or performance.

Upgrading personnel that perform a service through better hiring practices, training, and reward systems can differentiate services.

New product or service development calls for adding new products or services to an existing line. Often these new items appeal to people who were not in the original target market.

Market expansion is entering new geographic areas. A producer may initially launch a product in a local or regional area and gradually expand so that eventually the product is available nationally and even internationally. Service, retail, and restaurant firms can add stores in new locations.

Franchising is a popular way for service, retail, and restaurant firms to expand into new geographic areas. This involves granting the rights to own and operate the business in a prescribed manner to a franchisee. The franchisee pays an initial fee plus approximately 2% to 5% of all future sales to the franchiser.

AVID's future growth strategy involves differentiation and market expansion. Product development is being outsourced. This firm will be working on improvements in how Propell functions as well as exterior styling. In Years 2 and 3, the firm will also expand into geographic areas and stores where Propell is not available in Year 1.

Sales Forecast

One of the most difficult and important tasks that an entrepreneur must undertake for a start-up company is estimating sales. A *sales forecast* is a prediction of future sales revenue. Year 1 sales are especially difficult to estimate because there is no history that can be used for comparison. Producing an accurate forecast is very important because sales levels affect many areas of a business. Sales will determine production levels, the number of employees needed, the size of the office space that will be leased and many other factors. Projected sales levels also determine the amount of start-up capital that is needed and serve as the basis for financial statements.

If your business is a producer of products or a pure service firm, the following formula will be helpful in forecasting sales:

$$A \times B \times C = D$$

A = Average price per unit (or billing rate per hour for a pure service) charged to customers. (You determined this in the "Pricing Strategy" section earlier in this chapter.)

B = Number of units sold to each customer per year

C = Number of customers served per year

D = Total sales revenue in Year 1

AVID used this formula to forecast Propell's sales for Year 1. The marketing manager assumed that each pair of Propell would be sold to retailers for $89.50. This was discussed in the "Pricing Strategy" section earlier. It is estimated that each store will sell three pairs of Propell per week, which is 156 pairs per year per store (3 pairs times 52 weeks). AVID sales per store per year will, therefore, be $13,962 (156 pairs per year times $89.50 per pair). The industry analysis in chapter 1 indicated that there are 900 specialty retail stores in the United States that sell high-performance athletic shoes. The marketing manager estimated that 20% of these stores will decide to stock Propell. This means that 180 stores will be stocking the brand in Year 1 (900 stores times 20%). Projecting sales revenue involves multiplying A, B, and C in the formula. D will be sales for Year 1, which is $2,513,160 ($13,962 annual sales per store times 180 stores).

The same formula can be used to estimate sales for a retail store or restaurant; however, the information for each item is slightly different.

A = Average dollar sales per customer served. (This was determined in the "Pricing Strategy" section earlier in this chapter.)

B = Number of customers served per day

C = Number of days per year the firm is open for business

D = Total sales revenue in Year 1

Multiply A, B, and C together to get D, which will be your sales forecast for a year.

The total number of customers served per day at a restaurant is dependent on the number of meals served (breakfast, lunch, or dinner), number of seats and tables in the dining room (determined in chapter 2), and how many seats are occupied at each meal.

An example may help to illustrate how to project sales for a restaurant. Assume you are forecasting sales for the luncheon meal and the average check per customer is $10. There are 20 tables (80 seats) and all tables are occupied at lunch with an average of 2 people per table. Average daily sales for the luncheon meal would be $400 (20 tables times 2 people per table times $10 per person). If the restaurant is open 360 days per year, annual sales for lunch are $144,000 ($400 per day for lunch times 360 days).

An industry average for Year 1 sales for restaurants is $150 per square foot of leased space, assuming two meals are served per day. For example, if a restaurant were leasing 2,000 square feet, estimated annual sales would be $300,000 ($150 per foot times 2,000 feet). The industry average for Year 1 sales for retail stores is $200 per square foot of leased space. The amount of leased space needed for your business was determined in chapter 2.

Once Year 1 sales have been estimated, sales for Year 2 and 3 must be forecasted. Sales during these years are influenced by the future growth strategies that were discussed in the previous section. AVID SPORTS estimates sales in Year 2 will be 50% higher than Year 1 and sales in Year 3 will be 25% higher than in Year 2. Here are the figures that the company is using for planning purposes:

Year 1	Increase	Year 2	Increase	Year 3
$2,500,000	+50%	$3,750,000	+25%	$4,687,500

The industry averages for increases in sales for restaurants and retail stores in Years 2 and 3 are a 20% rise in Year 2 over Year 1 then a 10% rise in Year 3 over Year 2.

Concepts to Know

advertising

advertising appeals

advertising copy

atmospherics

brand name

channel of distribution

differentiation

direct channel of distribution

direct mail

distribution strategy

e-commerce

exclusive distribution

franchising

indirect channel of distribution

intensive distribution

magazines

market expansion

marketing

marketing plan

multiple channels

new product development

news release

newspapers

outdoor billboards

packaging

parity pricing

penetration pricing

pricing strategy

producers

product/service strategy

promotion

publicity

radio

sales agents

sales forecast

sales promotion

selective distribution

selling

skimming pricing

slogan

suppliers

telemarketers

television

Web site

Yellow Pages

Chapter 3 Issues: Marketing Plan

1. *Preparing for Team Meetings.* If you are a member of a team, refer to the section "Preparing for Team Meetings" in chapter 1. Follow the instructions on how to prepare for the meeting concerning the issues that follow.

2. *Product, Service, or Store Strategy.* Study this chapter. (Read all the issues that follow to determine which ones relate to your business concept.) Provide the brief business concept statement that was

developed in the Introduction section in the front of the book. Also provide the description of your target market that was developed for chapter 1. Explain your concept in detail. Clearly state how it is unique. Consider the desired features and benefits that you discovered in the customer survey and competitor analysis that was completed for chapter 1. If your concept involves producing a product, make a sketch of it if this will help explain the concept. Describe what it is made of and how it works. Identify a brand name and describe the packaging. If your concept is a service, describe all the services that will be offered during the first year. Why will your employees provide superior service? If your concept is a retail store, what specific merchandise will be sold and services offered? If your concept is a restaurant, construct an abbreviated menu. If your concept is a service that will be visited by customers, a retail store, or a restaurant, describe the store interior atmospherics and appearance of the building exterior. For all concepts, list and discuss five primary reasons why your business concept will be successful in the marketplace.

3. *Pricing Strategy*. What overall pricing strategy do you plan to use: penetration, parity, or skimming? Why? Consider the pricing data for competitors you gathered in chapter 1 of the business plan and the other factors affecting price that are mentioned in this chapter. Establish a price for your concept.

4. *Distribution Strategy*. If your concept involves producing a product, what geographic area will you serve: the local, regional, or national marketplace? Do you intend to use intensive, selective, or exclusive distribution? What types of outlets will stock your product? Refer to Exhibit 3.1 and diagram your channels of distribution. Describe the other aspects of your distribution strategy. Consider Exhibit 3.2. If your concept is a service, retail store, or restaurant, what days of the week and hours of the day are you open for business? Consider the needs and wants of your target market and the distribution strategy of competitors.

5. *Selling Strategy*. How will selling be used to promote your business? If your concept involves producing a product or a service that requires outside sales representatives, will you employ company salespeople

or independent sales agents? Indicate this in your channel(s) of distribution.

6. *Advertising Strategy*. What advertising media will be used to reach the target market efficiently? What percentage of sales will be allocated for advertising and sales promotion? Describe one advertisement for your concept for a type of media that you recommend. Include customer needs that will be exploited, the features you offer that appeal to the customers' needs, and visuals in the ad that reinforce the features. Consider the important needs of your target market that were identified in the survey conducted for chapter 1. Include a slogan that will be in the ad. If your business will have a Web site for promotional purposes, explain what information will be contained in it.

7. *Publicity Strategy*. How do you intend to get publicity for your concept? If you plan to organize or cosponsor an event, describe it.

8. *Sales Promotion Strategy*. What form(s) of sales promotion will be used to launch your business?

9. *Future Growth Strategies*. Describe how you will expand your business in the next 5 years. Be specific.

10. *Sales Forecast*. Determine projected sales revenue for your company for each of the first 3 years of operation. Include the percent increase for Years 2 and 3. Explain how these forecasts were determined. Secure approval of the forecasts from your instructor before working on chapter 4 of the business plan.

CHAPTER 4

Financial Plan

Looking Ahead

Upon completion of this chapter, you should be able to

1. explain the purpose of the financial plan;
2. prepare the following financial statements: income statement, cash-flow projection statement, and balance sheet;
3. determine the start-up capital requirements for a business;
4. choose appropriate sources of start-up capital; and
5. devise a repayment plan for start-up capital.

Purpose of the Financial Plan

Planning the financial affairs for a start-up firm is critical to success because many businesses fail during the first 3 years of operation due to poor financial plans and inadequate funding.

The *financial plan* section of the business plan outlines future sales revenue, expenses, and profit or loss. It also details what the firm will own and owe at the end of each year of operations. This chapter explains how to prepare financial statements for your business and determine how much funding will be required to launch and successfully operate the business during the start-up period. The following topics are presented in this chapter:

- Income Statement
- Cash-Flow Projection Statement
- Start-Up Capital Requirements
- Sources of Start-Up Capital

- Repayment Plan
- Balance Sheet

Most business plans provide financial statements for the first 3 years of operation because it is expected by financial institutions and investors. Your instructor, however, may determine that this level of detail is beyond the scope of the project and require financial statements for only the first year of operation. Ask your instructor about this.

Income Statement

An *income statement* is a financial statement indicating the projected sales revenue, expenses, and profit or loss for a business during a specified period of time. There are many items that are included in an income statement. These are illustrated in Exhibit 4.1, which is an income statement for AVID SPORTS for Year 1. Some of the comments in the statement under the column "Source or Method of Calculation" apply only to a producer of products. Refer to the discussion of each item to determine how to calculate amounts for your business.

Notice that the AVID income statement is for the first 12 months of the firm's operations. The dollar amounts are the sales and expenses for the entire year. Below is a discussion of typical items in the income statement.

Sales revenue is the income that a company receives for purchases by customers. You forecasted sales revenue in chapter 3 of this book. Projected sales for AVID in Year 1 are $2.5 million.

Cost of goods sold (COGS) is the cost incurred by producers to manufacture products that are sold to customers. It includes raw materials and component parts used in production and wages for production workers. Prorated costs of machines and factory overhead are also included. COGS does not include compensation for nonproduction employees. The following are some guidelines on calculating your COGS. Consider searching secondary sources for COGS averages in your industry.

- *Producer of products*: 60% of sales revenue = COGS. AVID's sales are projected to be $2.5 million. COGS is, therefore, $1.5 million (60% times $2.5 million).

Exhibit 4.1. Income Statement for AVID SPORTS
AVID SPORTS, INC.
Income Statement
January 1 through December 31, Year 1

		Source or method of calculation (for a firm that is a producer)
Sales revenue	$2,500,000	Sales were forecasted in chapter 3
Cost of goods sold (COGS)	1,500,000	60% of sales revenue
Gross profit	1,000,000	Sales revenue minus COGS
Fixed expenses		
Rent/lease of space	16,000	Calculated in chapter 2
Utilities and telephone	5,000	1000 square feet of space at $5/foot
Salary and wages	412,500	Calculated in chapter 2. See Exhibit 2.2
Depreciation	8,680	20% of $43,400. See Exhibit 2.3 in chapter 2
Office supplies	2,100	$300 for each of 7 employees
Insurance	125,000	5% of sales revenue above
Research and development	125,000	5% of sales revenue above
Interest on debt	10,000	10% interest for a $100,000 line of credit
Miscellaneous	25,000	1% of sales revenue above
TOTAL FIXED EXP.	729,280	Sum of all fixed expenses
Variable expenses		
Selling and distribution	250,000	5% of sales for selling and 5% for distribution
Advertising and promotion	250,000	10% of sales revenue above
Professional advisor fees	45,000	300 hours at $150/hour
TOTAL VARIABLE EXP.	545,000	Sum of all variable expenses
Total expenses	1,274,280	Sum of all fixed and variable expenses
Profit (or *loss*) before taxes	(274,280)	Gross profit minus total expenses (AVID is projecting a loss)
Corporate income taxes	0	Taxes are paid only if there is a profit
Net profit (or *loss*)	($274,280)	Net loss due to modest sales and high advertising and sales-promotion expenses in Year 1

- *Service firm*: There is no COGS for a pure service. A service that also sells products also must consider how much of sales revenues are from the service and products. Salary and wages for all service employees appear in the expenses section of the income statement.

- *Retail store*: 50% of sales revenue = COGS
- *Restaurant*: 60% of sales revenue = COGS. This includes the cost of food and chefs who prepare the food.

Gross profit is calculated by subtracting COGS from sales revenue. This is the amount a firm has available to cover operating expenses and make a profit. AVID's sales are $2.5 million and COGS are $1.5 million. Gross profit would be $1 million. Gross profit does not appear in the income statement for a pure service firm.

Fixed expenses do not vary with changes in production. For the purposes of this project, however, sales revenue will be the basis of computing fixed expenses because production levels are beyond the scope of our discussion. Typical fixed expense items are discussed later.

Rent/lease of space is the payment for office, warehouse, retail store, or restaurant space. The cost is usually based on the square feet of occupied space. Consider leasing space rather than purchasing a building. You have already calculated lease expense for your business in chapter 2.

Utilities and telephone expense includes the cost for heat (usually natural gas), electricity, water, and telephone. Assume this expense is $5 per square foot of your leased space. The leased space that AVID will occupy is 1,000 square feet. The utilities and telephone expense for the firm would be $5,000 per year.

Salary and wages expense includes compensation to employees including fringe benefits and payroll taxes. Salary and wages for people who work for outsourced firms are not included. You calculated this expense in chapter 2. If your business is a restaurant, the salary and wages for people who work in the kitchen are not to be included. Their compensation is already included in COGS. Salary and wages for all employees in a retail store are to be recorded here, including those for retail salespeople. Refer to Exhibit 2.2 for AVID's salary and wage expense.

Depreciation is the reduction in the value of fixed assets such as equipment, vehicles, leased-space improvements, and an e-commerce Web site that recognizes the asset has a limited useful life. A delivery vehicle or cash register, for example, has a limited life. The amount it depreciates in value each year is an expense. Complicated formulas are used to determine depreciation expense. For the purposes of this project, assume all equipment, vehicles, leased-space improvements, and an e-commerce Web site have a lifespan of 5 years and 20% of the purchase price is the yearly depreciation expense. For example, a cash register that costs $1,000 would have annual depreciation expense of $200 ($1,000 times 20%). At the end of 5 years it is fully depreciated. In chapter 2 you calculated the cost to purchase these items. Use the formula to calculate your annual depreciation expense. AVID plans on spending $43,400 for equipment (Exhibit 2.3). The firm does not have an investment in vehicles, leased-space improvements, or an e-commerce Web site. AVID's depreciation expense is $8,680 ($43,400 times 20%).

Office supplies expenses are items that employees use in their day-to-day activities. Many inexpensive products that are available at a store such as Office Max would be considered office supplies. Assume that your office supplies expense is $300 per employee. The number of employees in your firm was determined in chapter 2.

Insurance is needed by all businesses to protect against loss and liabilities. For example, a fire could destroy all the contents of a restaurant or a customer could fall and be injured. A producer needs product liability insurance in case someone is injured while using the product. Businesses also need insurance for workers who are injured on the job. Assume insurance expense for your business is 5% of annual sales revenue.

Research and development (R&D) is for the expense for developing new products and improving existing products. Services, retail stores, and restaurants typically do not have this expense. A Web-based business involving e-commerce can anticipate investing 20% of sales revenue on upgrading the Web site. R&D expenses can be high for high-tech products. AVID SPORTS will outsource this function and projects that annual R&D expense will be 5% of annual sales revenue because of the technical nature of its products.

Interest on debt is the fee paid to a lender such as a bank for borrowed funds. The lender does not receive ownership in the business. Later in this chapter there is a discussion of raising funds to start your business. A line of credit, which is a type of bank loan, is recommended. If you use this type of loan, you will have interest expense. Interest rates for loans to start-up businesses are usually high because of the risk involved to the lender. Assume the current interest rate is 10% of the amount of the loan.

If the loan is for $100,000, the annual interest expense will be $10,000. Also assume that payments are only for interest. Interest on debt expense cannot be determined until you decide whether a loan is needed. Loans are discussed later in this chapter.

Miscellaneous expenses are those that cannot be classified in one of the earlier areas. They include travel, entertainment, postage, maintenance, and unforeseen expenses. Allocate 1% of sales revenue for these expenses.

Variable expenses are the opposite of fixed expenses. They go up or down with changes in production. Since production levels are not a consideration in this project, sales revenue will be used to calculate fluctuations in variable expenses. The following are typical variable expenses.

Selling and distribution expense includes the cost of all compensation and overhead for sales personnel. Outside sales representatives are people who travel to customers and make presentations. The cost for distribution includes warehousing manufactured products and transporting them to customers. If you employ outside sales representatives or sales-agent firms to do the selling, assume sales expense is 5% of sales revenue. Plan on an additional 5% of sales for distribution if products are warehoused and delivered to customers. Assume there are no sales or distribution expense for a restaurant. Selling expense for a retail store is in "Salary and Wages."

Advertising and promotion expense is incurred to create ads and buy media. It also includes the cost of sales promotion that was discussed in chapter 3. Plan on spending 10% of annual sales revenue on advertising and sales promotion during Year 1 and 5% annually in subsequent years.

Professional advisor fees are paid to an attorney, consultant, or accounting firm. Most firms use professional advisors. This was discussed in the "Outsourcing" section in chapter 2. Determine what advisors you will need and the number of hours they will spend on your business during the year. Assume advisors receive $150 per hour for services. A small business can expect to spend $3,000 to $5,000 per year for these fees. AVID anticipates that professional fees will be $45,000 in Year 1. The amount is high because fees must be paid to an attorney and consultant.

Total expenses is the sum of fixed and variable expenses.

Profit (or loss) before taxes is calculated by subtracting total expenses from gross profit. Since a pure service has no COGS or gross profit, profit (or loss) before taxes is calculated by subtracting total expenses from sales revenue. Most start-up businesses do not show a profit during the first year of operation. AVID is projecting a $274,280 loss in Year 1.

Corporate income taxes are levied by local, state, and federal governments on the profits a corporation earns. If a firm breaks even or incurs a loss, no taxes are paid. Tax rates vary by state and local area. If you are assuming that your firm is a corporation and your company shows a profit, use 40% of profit before taxes as your corporate income tax expense.

Net profit (or loss) is calculated by subtracting corporate income taxes from profit before taxes. Dividends can be paid to stockholders if there are profits. The board of directors makes this determination. Board members may decide to keep profits in the business for expansion. This is called retained earnings, which appears in a firm's balance sheet.

Notice that the cost for purchasing equipment and vehicles, investments in leased-space improvements, and an e-commerce Web site do not appear in the income statement. These start-up costs, however, will appear in the balance sheet.

Cash-Flow Projection Statement

The lifeblood of any business is cash because it pays the bills and provides resources for expansion. The financial document that indicates a firm's cash position is the *cash-flow projection statement*. It shows cash inflows and outflows from operations. A firm must maintain a positive cash balance, or it will not be able to pay its expenses.

Cash inflows and outflows are affected when a firm receives actual payment from customers and pays its own bills. For the purposes of this project, assume your firm is using a cash method of accounting. This means that cash is received immediately when customers make purchases, such as in a retail store or restaurant. It also means that your firm pays cash for all purchases. This assumption will alleviate the need to explain accounts receivable and accounts payable and simplify calculations for the cash-flow projection statement and balance sheet.

The Year 1 cash-flow projection statement for AVID SPORTS is Exhibit 4.2. Following the exhibit is a discussion of each item that appears in the statement.

Investors and financial institutions require monthly cash-flow statements. Since the seasonality of monthly sales must be considered, the inflow and outflow of cash are affected. Ask your professor if a monthly statement is required.

Exhibit 4.2 indicates that AVID plans to end Year 1 with a cash shortage of $265,600 without the infusion of cash from a bank loan or the sale of stock. The discussion that follows explains how this was calculated.

Cash inflows from operations are cash that is actually received by a company. The only cash inflow that AVID will have is from sales revenue. AVID will be selling the Propell running shoe to retailers. Sales revenue is recorded in the income statement (Exhibit 4.1).

Cash outflows from operations are cash that actually leaves a company. This includes COGS for all firms except pure services, fixed expenses, and variable expenses from the income statement. Depreciation expense

Exhibit 4.2. Cash-Flow Projection Statement for AVID SPORTS for Year 1

AVID SPORTS, INC.
Cash-Flow Projection Statement
January 1 Through December 31, Year 1

		Source or method of calculation (For a firm that is a producer)
Cash inflows from operations		
Sales revenue—Year 1	$2,500,000	Sales revenue from the income statement
Total cash inflows	2,500,000	Same as above
Cash outflows from operations		
Cost of goods sold	1,500,000	COGS from the income statement
Fixed expenses	729,280	Fixed expenses from the income statement
Deduct depreciation expense	(8,680)	Depreciation expenses from the income statement. It is an expense on paper but does not require an outlay of cash
Variable expenses	545,000	Variable expenses from the income statement
Total cash outflows	2,765,600	Sum of COGS, fixed expenses, and variable expenses. Depreciation is deducted from the subtotal.
Net cash surplus (or shortage)	($265,600)	Total cash inflows minus outflows (AVID projects a net cash shortage)

is also an item used in calculating cash outflows. Recall that it is a means of accounting for the fact that assets such as computers and vehicles have a limited life span. Each year, depreciation is recorded as an expense in the income statement until the cost of the original purchase is fully expensed. Unlike other expenses, however, depreciation is not a cash outflow. Money does not leave the company to pay for depreciation, so the amount of depreciation in the income statement must be deducted from cash outflows. AVID must reduce projected cash outflows by $8,680, which is its projected depreciation expense in the income statement.

Net cash surplus (or shortage) is determined by subtracting total cash outflows from total cash inflows. AVID's net cash shortage from operations is projected to be $265,600 for Year 1. This condition means that the firm will not be able to pay its bills unless start-up capital is secured from a bank or investors.

Start-Up Capital Requirements

An important question that the entrepreneur must answer is, "How much money is needed to begin operations of a new business and pay bills through the end of Year 1?" This is *start-up capital*, and it must be estimated and secured before operations begin. The anticipated start-up capital requirements for AVID SPORTS including cash needed to end Year 1 with a positive cash balance are shown in Exhibit 4.3.

Exhibit 4.3 indicates that AVID needs $434,000 in start-up capital (funds from a loan or the sale of stock) to pay for its start-up costs and provide for its cash needs. The discussion that follows explains how this figure was calculated.

AVID's equipment costs of $43,400 were determined in chapter 2 (Exhibit 2.3). The company does not have leased-space improvements or e-commerce Web site costs.

Inventory is a start-up cost for all firms except pure services because it must be on hand and available for sale on the first day of operation. Producers and retail stores should plan on having enough initial inventory for 1 month of sales. This can be calculated by taking the COGS for Year 1 indicated on the income statement and dividing it by 12 months. A restaurant only needs 1 week's supply of inventory on hand to

Exhibit 4.3. Start-Up Capital Requirements Statement for AVID SPORTS

		Source or Method of Calculation (for a firm that is a producer)
Equipment and vehicles	$43,400	Determined in chapter 2 (Exhibit 2.3)
Leased-space improvements	0	The office space that AVID will occupy does not require any remodeling.
E-commerce Web site	0	AVID will not have this type of site in Year 1
Initial inventory	125,000	Average cost of goods sold for 1 month from the income statement ($1,500,000 divided by 12 months)
Total start-up costs	$168,400	Sum of the above items
Net cash shortage	265,600	Net cash shortage from the cash-flow projection statement (Exhibit 4.2)
Total start-up capital needed	$434,000	Sum of total start-up costs and net cash shortage. (If needed net cash is a surplus, subtract start-up costs and cash surplus.)
Cash from a loan and sale of stock (start-up capital)	500,000	Proceeds from the $100,000 line of credit and sale of $400,000 in common stock discussed later in the chapter
Projected cash balance— end of Year 1	$66,000	Cash from loan/stock minus start-up capital needed. (This is the Year 1 "Cash" account balance that will appear in the balance sheet.)

begin operations, since many items are perishable and food wholesalers deliver frequently. For example, if the COGS in the income statement is $100,000, inventory would be $1,923 ($100,000 divided by 52 weeks). A pure service does not have inventory.

Funding for AVID's start-up costs of $168,400 is enough to open it doors; however, it is not sufficient to end Year 1 with a positive cash balance. The cash-flow projection statement (Exhibit 4.2) indicated the firm needs $265,600 in additional cash to end the year with a positive cash balance. Therefore, a minimum of $434,000 of start-up capital must be raised ($168,400 plus $265,600) from a loan or the sale of stock to ensure the company has enough money to end the year with cash on hand to begin Year 2. AVID plans to raise $500,000 in start-up capital, which is discussed in the next section. Exhibit 4.3 indicates this will result in having a positive cash balance of $66,000 at the end of Year 1.

Sources of Start-Up Capital

How does an entrepreneur raise the start-up capital needed to launch a business? There are three primary sources: self-funding, loans, and the sale of stock in a corporation.

Self-funding is using funds from personal assets such as a savings account, loan on the equity in a home, and credit cards.

Debt financing is money that is borrowed. The principal of the loan plus interest must be repaid to the lender. The lender does not receive ownership in the business. Loans can be secured from family members, friends, or a bank. Banks are very hesitant to grant loans to start-up businesses due to the risk involved. Often they require borrowers to pledge personal assets to secure loans. This is *collateral*. If borrowers default on loans, they must forfeit the assets to the bank.

The *Small Business Administration (SBA)* is a federal agency that helps businesses secure loans from banks. If the SBA determines that a start-up business is likely to succeed, it may authorize a guaranteed loan through a bank. If the firm defaults on the loan, the SBA will reimburse the bank up to 90% of the outstanding principal. Banks are more likely to grant a loan that is through the SBA because its risk is substantially reduced.

There are many types of loans available to businesses. A *line of credit* from a bank was discussed earlier. It is an agreement between a company and a bank where the bank agrees to provide funds as needed up to a specific amount. It typically does not have a maturity date. The bank continues to make funds available provided the company is doing well.

A *long-term loan* is another type of debt financing. It is a debt with a specific maturity date. Monthly payments are made that include interest and a portion of the principal. This type of debt is considered long-term because the principal does not have to be repaid within 1 year. Long-term loans may be secured from family and friends of the founders or a bank.

Equity financing involves the sale of stock in a corporation. A firm must have the corporate form of ownership to sell stock. Investors who purchase stock receive ownership in the company. The amount invested is not repaid like a loan, and there are no guarantees that investors will get back what they initially paid for the stock. Stock in a new venture is not usually sold to the general public through a stock exchange; in this case, shares are sold privately. Founders often purchase stock when a company is formed. There are also people who invest in start-up businesses. They are called *angel investors*. They are not associated with the company and may be family members or friends of the founders.

There are different types of stock, but most new businesses issue common stock. Members of the board of directors determine an arbitrary number of *authorized shares* when a corporation is formed. AVID is authorizing 100,000 shares of common stock. *Issued shares* are ones that are sold and outstanding. AVID plans to sell 16,000 shares of the 100,000 that are authorized to provide cash to launch the business. The remaining 84,000 shares are available to be sold at a later date. The initial price per share is also arbitrary. AVID's board of directors decided the price for its common stock should be $25 per share.

In the previous section it was determined that AVID plans to raise $500,000 for start-up costs and cash needed to end Year 1 with a positive cash balance (see Exhibit 4.3). The founders plan to raise these funds through the following means:

- $100,000 line of credit from a bank that is guaranteed by the SBA. The interest rate will be 10%.
- $400,000 through the sale of common stock. 16,000 shares will be sold at $25 per share—10,000 shares to AVID's four founders (2,500 shares to each founder), and 6,000 shares to angel investors.

The founders will retain controlling interest in the company because collectively they own more than half of the shares that will be sold.

Repayment Plan

There is substantial risk for investors and banks that provide funds to a start-up business. Before investors purchase stock, they want to know the projected growth rate of a business and the net worth or value of the firm in the future. Banks want to be assured that the business will have sufficient positive cash flow to make payments on a loan. A business plan must address these issues in a *repayment plan*.

The best way to illustrate repayment is to construct an income statement, cash-flow projection statement, and balance sheet that indicate the financial status of the company for the first 3 years of operation. Investors and financial institutions require this. Ask your instructor if this level of detail is needed.

Balance Sheet

A *balance sheet* is a financial statement that lists a firm's assets, liabilities, and stockholders' equity on a given date. It shows what a firm owns, owes, and how much it is worth. The date is usually the last day of a firm's operating year, so it is a snapshot of a firm's financial position on that date. The equation that shows the relationship between the major sections in the balance sheet is

$$Assets = Liabilities + Stockholders' Equity$$
$$(Owns) = (Owes) + (Net\ Worth)$$

Exhibit 4.4 is a balance sheet for AVID SPORTS for the first year of operation. The dollar amount for each item reflects its status on the last day of Year 1. It assumes that a $100,000 line of credit is secured and the $400,000 sale of stock is successful. Comments under the column "Source or Method of Calculation" are for a producer of products. Methods of calculation may be different if your business is a retail store, restaurant, or service. Refer to the discussion of each item that follows to determine the figures for your business.

Assets are any items that a business owns that have value. Typical business assets are discussed later.

Current assets include cash and items that can be converted into cash or consumed within 1 year.

Cash includes petty cash that is in the cash register of a store or restaurant and funds deposited in a business checking or savings account. The amount of cash that is reflected in the balance sheet should be the

Exhibit 4.4. *Balance Sheet for AVID SPORTS*

AVID SPORTS, INC.
Balance Sheet
December 31, Year 1 (Last Day of Year 1)

Source or Method of Calculation
(For a firm that is a producer)

Assets

Current assets

Cash	$66,000	Projected end-of-year cash balance from Exhibit 4.3
Inventory	125,000	Average COGS for 1 month ($1.5 million divided by 12)

Fixed assets

Equipment	43,400	Original cost of equipment (see Exhibit 2.3 in chapter 2)
Vehicles	0	No vehicles; AVID is outsourcing distribution
Leased-space improvements	0	Space the firm will lease is in move-in condition
E-commerce Web site	0	This type of site will not be used in Year 1
Less accumulated depreciation	(8,680)	Depreciation expense from the income statement (negative number)
Total assets	$225,720	Sum of current and fixed assets minus accumulated depreciation

Liabilities

Current liabilities

Line of credit	100,000	SBA guaranteed line of credit through a bank

Long-term liabilities

Loan payable	0	AVID is using a line of credit, not a long-term loan
Total liabilities	100,000	Sum of all current and long-term liabilities

Stockholders' equity

Common stock

16,000 shares at

$25/share	$400,000	10,000 shares to founders and 6,000 to angel investors
Retained earnings	(274,280)	Net loss in Year 1 from AVID income statement (if a company earns a profit, this would be a positive number)
Total stockholders' equity	125,720	Common stock above minus retained earnings (add retained earnings to common stock, if company earns a profit)
Total liabilities and stockholders' equity	$225,720	Sum of total liabilities and stockholders' equity (must equal amount for total assets above)

projected cash balance at the end of the year that appears in the calculations for start-up capital requirements. Refer to Exhibit 4.3. Note that AVID projects a positive cash balance at the end of Year 1 of $66,000. This amount appears in the firm's balance sheet as cash.

Inventory is the cost of raw materials or component parts that will be used in manufacturing and eventually sold as finished products and products that are already available for sale. Firms that are pure services do not have inventory. If your firm is a producer or retail store, plan on having enough inventory for 1 month of sales to begin Year 2. However, calculate inventory volume based on COGS, not sales revenue, because sales revenue is not the cost of the inventory. AVID's projected COGS in its income statement (Exhibit 4.1) is $1,500,000. The average COGS for 1 month would be $125,000 ($1,500,000 divided by 12 months). The amount for inventory that appears in the balance sheet is $125,000. If your business is a restaurant, use average *weekly* COGS for inventory. Many items in a restaurant are perishable and food wholesalers deliver frequently. One week's supply of inventory for most items is sufficient to serve customers without going out-of-stock. For example, if the COGS in the income statement for Year 1 were $100,000, inventory in the balance sheet would be $1,923 ($100,000 divided by 52 weeks).

Fixed assets are items that are purchased for use in a company and are not intended to be sold. The useful life of a fixed asset is greater than 1 year.

Equipment was determined in chapter 2.

Vehicles were determined in chapter 2. AVID does not have any vehicles because delivery of its products will be outsourced.

Leased-space improvements were determined in chapter 2. AVID does not have remodeling expense because the office space it will lease is in move-in condition.

E-commerce Web site was determined in chapter 2. Only a Web-based business site that can accept orders and payments from customers will have this asset in the balance sheet.

Accumulated depreciation is the depreciation expense that fixed assets have been charged since they were purchased. These fixed assets include equipment, vehicles, leased-space improvements, and an e-commerce Web site. The fixed assets needed to start AVID SPORTS will cost $43,400. This was illustrated in chapter 2, Exhibit 2.3. Assume equipment is depreciated over a 5-year period and the depreciation amount is 20% per year. The depreciation expense for Year 1 that appears in AVID's income statement (Exhibit 4.1) is $8,680 ($43,400 times 20%). Depreciation for Year 2 would be added to depreciation in Year 1 to determine *accumulated depreciation* in Year 2. Accumulated depreciation is shown as a negative number (in parentheses) in the balance sheet because it is a reduction in the value of fixed assets.

Total assets are calculated by adding current assets and fixed assets and subtracting accumulated depreciation. AVID projects that it will have assets totaling $225,720 at the end of Year 1.

Liabilities are obligations the firm has to suppliers and creditors. Following are typical items that appear in this section of a balance sheet.

Current liabilities are funds a firm owes to others that must be paid within one year.

A *line of credit* is a formal agreement between a company and a bank where the bank agrees to provide funds as needed up to a specific amount. An advantage to this type of loan is that it does not have a maturity date. Funds are available provided the company is doing well and the bank wants to continue the line of credit. The business does not have to secure the full amount of the loan but only what it needs when cash is in short supply. The amount of funds outstanding, therefore, may fluctuate throughout the year. Interest is paid only for the funds a business has outstanding. AVID SPORTS plans to secure a $100,000 line of credit.

Long-term liabilities are funds owed to creditors that do not have to be paid within 1 year. Loan payable is a long-term liability.

Loan payable is a debt owed to creditors such as a bank and has a specific maturity date. The loan does not have to be paid off within 1 year, and the creditor does not receive ownership in the business. Earlier in this chapter you determined if a loan is needed for start-up capital.

Total liabilities are the sum of current and long-term liabilities. AVID's total liabilities will be $100,000.

Stockholders' equity is the financial investment that stockholders in a corporation made plus the profits (if any) that have been retained in the business and not distributed to stockholders in the form of dividends. Stockholders' equity is the net worth (or value) of a company because it is the difference between the assets of a company (what it owns) and liabilities (what it owes). Common stock and retained earnings appear in this section of the balance sheet.

Common stock represents ownership in the corporation held by stockholders. This was discussed under "Start-Up Capital Requirements" earlier in this chapter. Refer to it and your cash-flow projection statement to determine the amount of common stock that should appear in your balance sheet. Assume the sale of stock will be successful. AVID plans to raise $400,000 from the sale of stock.

Retained earnings are the net profit (if any) after corporate income taxes and dividends have been paid to stockholders. They are the funds that are kept in the business for future growth. Retained earnings are a negative number if your company will incur a loss, and it is recorded in parentheses on the balance sheet. It is a positive number if profit is realized. The income statement for AVID (Exhibit 4.1) indicates that the company will incur a $274,280 loss in Year 1. This amount appears in its balance sheet as negative retained earnings.

Total stockholders' equity is the sum of the value of common stock and retained earnings. Retained earnings will be a negative number if your firm is projecting a loss in the income statement. AVID is projecting a loss in Year 1. Stockholders' equity was calculated by subtracting the loss of $274,280 from $400,000 in common stock. If retained earnings were a positive number (AVID made a profit in Year 1), these figures would be added.

Total liabilities and stockholders' equity is calculated by adding total liabilities and total stockholders' equity. This amount must equal total assets reflected in the balance sheet (Assets = Liabilities + Stockholders' Equity). Notice in Exhibit 4.4 that AVID's assets at the end of Year 1 are $225,720. This is the same amount for total liabilities plus stockholders' equity.

Concepts to Know

accumulated depreciation	gross profit
advertising and promotion expense	income statement
angel investors	interest on debt
assets	inventory
balance sheet	issued shares of stock
cash	liabilities
cash inflows	line of credit
cash outflows	long-term liabilities
cash-flow projection	net profit (or loss)
common stock	professional advisor fees
corporate income taxes	retained earnings
cost of goods sold (COGS)	sales revenue
current assets	self-funding
current liabilities	selling and distribution expense
debt financing	small business administration (SBA)
depreciation expense	start-up capital
equity financing	statement
financial plan	stockholders' equity
fixed assets	variable expenses
fixed expenses	

Chapter 4 Issues: Financial Plan

1. *Preparing for Team Meetings.* If you are a member of a team, refer to the section "Preparing for Team Meetings" in chapter 1. Follow the instructions on preparing for the team meeting concerning the issues that follow.

2. *Income Statement.* Study this chapter. Develop an income statement for your business. Consider the format in Exhibit 4.1.

3. *Cash-Flow Projection Statement.* Develop a cash-flow projection statement indicating inflows and outflows of cash. Consider the format in Exhibit 4.2.

4. *Start-Up Capital Requirements.* Review the income and cash-flow projection statements. Determine how much start-up capital is needed to begin operations and ensure that there is sufficient cash to operate the business during the first year without incurring a negative cash position. Construct a start-up capital requirement statement. Consider the format in Exhibit 4.3. What sources of start-up capital are you seeking? Indicate how much capital you plan to raise through a loan and/or the sale of stock. If a loan is planned, indicate the type and amount of the loan. If stock will be used to finance the business, indicate how many shares will be authorized and how many will be sold. Also note the price per share at which the stock will be sold.

5. *Repayment Plan.* How will start-up capital be repaid?

6. *Balance Sheet.* Develop a balance sheet for your operation. Consider the format in Exhibit 4.4.

APPENDIX

Written Business Plan and Oral Presentation

Looking Ahead

Upon completion of this chapter, you should be able to

1. describe all the sections of a business plan including the executive summary,
2. write a complete business plan proposal for a new business, and
3. develop and deliver an effective oral presentation of a business plan using PowerPoint slides and other visual aids.

Purpose and Overview of the Business Plan

In the first chapter of the book, you learned that a *business plan* is a written proposal that describes how a business will be structured and operated during a specified period, which is usually 1 or more years. It was mentioned that there are two reasons for creating a plan for a new business: first, to convince banks and potential investors to provide the necessary start-up capital to launch a business and, second, to serve as a road map to establish and operate the business.

Throughout this book you have explored the contents of a business plan. In chapter 1, you completed an industry, customer, and competitor analysis. The target market was identified, and the needs of the target market were determined through the use of a market research survey. In chapter 2, you described how the company would be structured and staffed, where it will be located, and detailed the space the business will occupy. Product, pricing, distribution, and promotion strategies were outlined in chapter 3. Chapter 4 involved constructing financial statements for the proposed business. Start-up capital requirements and sources of capital were also identified. It is now time to learn how to write the business plan proposal and conduct an oral presentation of the plan. The following topics are presented in this chapter:

- Executive Summary
- Sections in the Written Business Plan
- Written Plan Checklist
- Sections in the Oral Presentation
- Visual Aids for the Oral Presentation
- Oral Presentation Checklist
- Nondisclosure Agreement

Executive Summary

The *executive summary* is the last section of the business plan that needs to be discussed. It is the introduction of the plan that provides a very concise overview of the proposed business. The executive summary highlights the most critical information that bankers and potential investors want to know before investing in a business. It is no more than two pages in length and is written after all other sections of the plan have been completed. "Executive Summary" appears at the top of the first page. The following is a description of the content in each section of the executive summary:

Purpose and overview. State that the purpose of the business plan is to request funding to launch the business. Provide the name of your company, names of the founders, and the business concept statement.

Opportunity analysis. State the industry in which you will compete as well as current and projected industry sales. Briefly mention important strengths and weaknesses of competitors. Provide a brief description of your intended target market.

Organization plan. Mention the form of ownership chosen (sole proprietorship, partnership, or corporation) and present your company vision statement. Explain what functions will be outsourced. Clarify how many full- and part-time employees will be needed. Disclose where the business will be located.

Marketing plan. Briefly explain your concept and how it is unique. Explain the overall pricing strategy (penetration, parity, or skimming strategy). If your firm is a producer, explain what stores will stock your product. Briefly explain how promotion will be used to create awareness of your product or business and the plans you have for future growth.

Financial plan. Provide the following financial information for Year 1 (and Year 2 and 3, if required by your instructor): (a) projected sales, (b) profit (or loss), (c) net cash surplus (or shortage) from operations, and (d) total start-up capital needed to launch the business. Explain what sources of funding you are seeking (loan and/or sale of stock).

Summary. In this section, summarize the plan in one paragraph. List and discuss the most important reasons why your business is an excellent investment opportunity. Urge the reader to study the entire business plan.

Sections in the Written Business Plan

The following is a discussion of the content of the written plan. Assume readers of the plan are potential private investors and representatives of banks that are authorized to grant loans. The goal of the written plan is to convince them to provide the start-up capital needed to launch your business.

Cover Page

The cover page should include the following information:

Business Plan for (Name of company)
Founders: (Name of each person who worked on the plan)
Consultant: (Names of your instructor and educational institution, if
     appropriate)
(Date the plan was submitted)

Table of Contents

The table of contents should be on a separate sheet of paper. "Table of Contents" appears at the top of the page. Include the following section numbers and titles and page numbers for each section.

Executive Summary

Refer to the earlier section for what should be in this section.

Section 1: Opportunity Analysis

1.1. Industry and Customer Analysis. State the industry in which you will compete. Briefly provide any relevant industry and customer information that was gathered for this section of the plan. Of particular interest to investors is the past, current, and projected sales for the industry. Provide citations for references that were used in this section in the Bibliography that appears at the end of the plan.

1.2. Competitor Analysis. Briefly profile the competitor(s) and list their major strengths and weaknesses. Provide references in the bibliography at the end of the plan for citations in this section.

1.3. Target Market. Define your target market using relevant demographic, geographic, and psychographic characteristics. Consider the format used in Exhibit 1.3 in chapter 1. Explain why you have chosen this segment.

1.4. Market Research. Explain the nature of your market research study and present the findings. Consider the format in Exhibit 1.5 in chapter 1. Direct the reader to the "Supporting Documents" section at the end of the plan where your questionnaire is provided.

Section 2: Organization Plan

2.1. Company Name and Vision. Provide your company name and a one- or two-sentence vision statement for the company. Explain why these were chosen.

2.2. Form of Ownership. Confirm the form of ownership that was chosen and explain the reasons for this choice.

2.3. Days and Hours of Operation. State when you will be open for business.

2.4. Outsourcing. Explain what functions (if any) will be outsourced.

2.5. Staffing and Management Team. List the staff and management positions in your firm. Clarify which employees will be full and part time. Refer the reader to the "Supporting Documents" section for the organizational chart.

2.6. Employee Compensation. Outline the employee compensation expense for Year 1. Consider the format in Exhibit 2.2 in chapter 2.

2.7. Business Location. Mention the proposed location for the business and why it was chosen.

2.8. Equipment and Space Requirements. Discuss the size and cost of leased space needed for the business. List the equipment and other start-up items needed and total costs. Tell the reader that a detailed break-down of equipment costs is in the "Supporting Documents" section of the plan. Also direct the reader to the "Supporting Documents" section for the diagram of the floor plan.

Section 3: Marketing Plan

3.1. Product, Service, or Store Strategy. Explain your business concept in detail. State how it is superior to competitors.

3.2. Pricing Strategy. State your price and why it is realistic.

3.3. Distribution Strategy. Explain the plans for this area. If you have a diagram of your channels of distribution, direct the reader to it in the "Supporting Documents" section.

3.4. Promotion Strategy. Discuss what you plan to do in selling, advertising, publicity, and sales promotion.

3.5. Future Growth Strategies. Briefly discuss your plans for the future.

3.6. Sales Forecast. Provide projected annual sales for Years 1, 2, and 3. Explain how they were determined. Indicate the percentage of growth for Years 2 and 3.

Section 4: Financial Plan

4.1. Income Statement. Present only a summary of this statement that includes the following: (a) sales revenue, (b) cost of goods sold (COGS), (c) total fixed expenses, (d) total variable expenses, and (e) net profit (or loss) after taxes. Tell the reader that the complete income statement is in the "Supporting Documents" section of the plan.

4.2. Cash-Flow Projection Statement. Provide only a summary of this statement by stating the following: (a) total cash inflows, (b) total cash outflows, and (c) net cash surplus (or shortage) from operations. Direct the reader to the "Supporting Documents" section for the complete cash flow projection statement.

4.3. Start-Up Capital Requirements. Provide only a summary by stating the following: (a) total start-up costs, (b) cash surplus (or shortfall) from operations, and (c) total start-up capital needed. Direct the reader to the complete list of start-up capital requirements in the "Supporting Documents" section.

4.4. Sources of Start-Up Capital. Explain the types of start-up capital you need (loan and/or sale of stock) to launch the business and how much is being requested for each type.

4.5. Repayment Plan. Explain how start-up capital funding will be repaid.

4.6. Balance Sheet. Present only a summary of this statement by including the following: (a) total assets, (b) total liabilities, and (c) total stockholders' equity. Refer the reader to the "Supporting Documents" sections for the complete balance sheet.

Summary

Summarize the business plan in one paragraph. List and discuss five very convincing reasons why your business concept will be successful. Urge the reader to invest in your business.

Supporting Documents

Include a separate page that lists the supporting documents (SD) followed by the actual documents. "Supporting Documents" should appear at the top of the title page.

Include the following documents:

SD.1   Market Research Questionnaire (chapter 1; consider the format in Exhibit 1.4)

SD.2   Organizational Chart (chapter 2; consider the format in Exhibit 2.1)

SD.3   Equipment, Leased-Space Improvements, and Web Site Costs (chapter 2; consider the format in Exhibit 2.3)

SD.4   Floor Plan (chapter 2; consider the format in Exhibit 2.4)

SD.5   Income Statement (chapter 4; consider the format in Exhibit 4.1)

SD.6   Cash-Flow Projection Statement (chapter 4; consider the format in Exhibit 4.2)

SD.7   Start-Up Capital Requirements Statement (chapter 4; consider the format in Exhibit 4.3)

SD.8   Balance Sheet (chapter 4; consider the format in Exhibit 4.4)

Bibliography

On a separate page, provide bibliographic references for the sources that were used in the development of the business plan. "Bibliography" should appear at the top of the page.

Written Plan Checklist

Several factors will be considered in evaluating your written business plan. These are listed on the following page. Use this checklist to evaluate the report before it is submitted. Confirm with your instructor the page limit including the "Supporting Documents" and "Bibliography" sections and whether the report should be single or double spaced.

Content

Coverage of sections, clarity, referred the reader to "Supporting Documents" section, within page limitation

Format

Word processed; bold section headings with consistent font; 12-point font used in narrative portions; consistent margins, indenting, and spacing; page numbers on all pages; page numbers in the "Table of Contents" correspond to those in the report

Writing Style

Clear; concise; smooth flow; proper paragraphing, sentence structure, grammar and word usage

Professionalism

Appearance, spelling, punctuation, free of typographic errors, proper use of capitalization, written as if reader is a potential investor

Be sure to have several people proofread the report before it is submitted.

Sections in the Oral Presentation

Entrepreneurs who are seeking start-up capital often speak to groups of potential investors. This calls for an oral presentation of the business plan. The goal of the presentation is to convince potential investors to consider investing in the business and study the written plan after the oral presentation. The structure and content of the oral presentation is similar to the written plan with a few exceptions. Following is a discussion of the content of the oral presentation.

The *introduction of the oral presentation* should be designed to establish a rapport with investors (the audience) to get their attention and to preview the topics that will be discussed. There are five parts to the introduction:

1. Begin with a greeting to make the audience feel welcome and form a connection with them. Two examples are "Good morning (or afternoon)" or "Thank you for attending our presentation today."
2. Build anticipation and get their attention by asking a provocative or rhetorical question or telling a brief story related to your business concept.
3. Introduce those who prepared and are participating in the presentation.
4. State the purpose of the presentation, which is to provide an overview of your investment opportunity.
5. Preview the topics that will be presented in the report by providing your business concept statement then listing and briefly discussing the four sections of the business plan.

The introduction should not take more than 2 minutes.

The *body of the oral presentation* contains your analysis and recommendations. It presents essentially the same information that is in the body of the written report; however, some information is omitted due to time constraints. All sections in the body of the written report outlined earlier should be included in the oral presentation except for those noted in the following section. Section numbers (e.g., 1.1, 1.2, etc.) correspond to those in the written report discussed earlier. All items in the "Supporting Documents" section of the written plan are not to be presented in the presentation itself. They are distributed as handouts before the question and answer period.

Section 1: Opportunity Analysis

1.1.   Omit citations of sources, since they are in the bibliography of the written plan.
1.2.   Omit citations of sources.

Section 2: Organization Plan

2.2.   Omit the reasons why you chose the form of ownership.
2.3.   Omit the section on days and hours of operation.
2.6.   Omit employee compensation section.
2.8.   Omit equipment and space requirement section.

Section 3: Marketing Plan

3.4.   Make no changes in the content of the written report, except discuss only the most important aspects of your promotion strategy.

Section 4: Financial Plan

Make no changes in the content of the written report but only summarize major items.

The goal of the *summary of the oral presentation* is to briefly summarize the presentation, restate compelling reasons for investing in your business, and ask investors to provide the funding needed to launch the business. The following are six parts of the summary:

1. Provide a transition from the body of the presentation to the summary, such as "Let's review what we have shared with you today"
2. Review the presentation by providing your business concept statement and what start-up capital you are requesting
3. List and briefly discuss five important reasons why your business will be successful
4. Urge the investors to seriously consider investing in the business
5. Thank the investors for being present
6. Solicit questions and comments after distributing the supporting documents handout

The summary should not take more than 2 minutes excluding the time for questions.

Visual Aids for the Oral Presentation

People learn more from what they see than what they hear. This is why it is very important to use multiple *visual aids* throughout the oral presentation. Visual aids can be overhead transparencies, computer-generated slides such as PowerPoint, handouts, props, or other devices. When planning the presentation, focus on how the visual elements will reinforce each point and effectively convey them to your audience.

The font for visual aids that are projected on a screen must be large enough to be seen from the back of the room. PowerPoint slides require 36-point font or larger. *Bullet points* should be used for each idea rather than compete sentences. A bullet point is a word or short phrase that summarizes an idea. The following image could be used to communicate AVID's target market:

Target Market

- Age 25–54
- Male or female
- College degree
- $50,000+ household income
- Serious runner

There are two items in the presentation where bullet points should not be used: the business concept statement and the company vision statement. These should be conveyed word for word in their entirety.

There should be a minimum of one visual aid that is projected on a screen for each minute in the presentation, preferably more. The introduction, for example, could have three visuals. The first would be the title slide containing the name of your company and the name(s) of the person (or persons) that developed the plan. A second slide would be used for the business concept statement. The preview of the main issues in the body of the presentation requires a third slide. All major topics require a visual aid and all major ideas require one or more bullet points.

Before you begin the presentation, distribute hardcopy of your PowerPoint slides to each person in attendance.

Oral Presentation Checklist

Several factors will be considered in evaluating your oral presentation. These are listed on the following page. Ask your instructor what the time limit for the presentation is and whether professional business attire is required.

Content of the Presentation

- *Introduction.* Greeting; attention-getter/anticipation builder; introduction of the presenters; purpose of the presentation; preview of the topics
- *Body of the presentation.* Coverage of sections; clarity; referring audience to supporting documents
- *Summary.* Transition to the summary section; review of the major points; reasons why the business will be successful; make case for audience to invest in the business; thanking the audience; solicitation of questions and comments
- *Supporting documents (handouts, not slides).* Market research questionnaire; organizational chart; equipment; leased-space improvements and Web site costs; floor plan; income statement; cash-flow projection statement; start-up capital requirements statement; balance sheet

Delivery of the Presentation

- *Organization.* Order of topics presented; smooth flow
- *Vocal expression.* Sufficient volume to be heard; conversational delivery; proper enunciation; enthusiastic tone; free of objectionable mannerisms ("um," "ah," "and um," "okay," "like," gum chewing)
- *Nonverbal communication.* Maintained eye contact; use of hand gestures and body movements; smile; sustained good posture
- *Use of visual aids.* Number of visuals; use of bullet points; readability from back of the room; consistent layout and font; free of typographic errors
- *Professionalism.* Knowledge of information; self-confidence; word usage; spoke to audience as if they were investors; business dress; within time limitation

Practice the entire presentation several times using visual aids. The checklist above will be helpful in evaluating the presentation.

Nondisclosure Agreement

Ideas for new business ventures cannot be patented or trademarked. How does an entrepreneur protect an idea from being stolen? While there are no guarantees, one way to retain the rights is to use a *nondisclosure agreement*. The purpose of the agreement is to inform the recipient of information (potential investor) that rights to the idea remain the property of the person offering the idea. The form should be completed and signed by both parties before any information is revealed. Nondisclosure agreement forms are available in some books on business plans. An attorney would also have them.

Concepts to Know

bullet points	introduction, body, and summary of the
business plan	oral presentation
executive summary	nondisclosure agreement
	visual aids

Written Plan and Oral Presentation Issues

1. Go to the Web site http://www.bplans.com. Read several business plans to gain an understanding of how plans are written. Generally, the majority of the plan body consists of narrative description. Also, financial statements are not in the body of most plans because they appear in the "Supporting Documents" section at the end of the plan. Use the section headings in a business plan that are noted in this chapter when writing your plan, not headings in the Web site.

2. Study this chapter. Write a complete business plan proposal for your concept.

3. Prepare to deliver a persuasive oral presentation of your business plan using PowerPoint slides and other visual aids.

Index

CPSIA information can be obtained
at www.ICGtesting.com
Printed in the USA
LVOW04s0721080116

469753LV00029B/1018/P